False Black Power?

FALSE BLACK POWER?

><

Jason L. Riley

NEW
THREATS TO
FREEDOM
SERIES

Templeton Press
300 Conshohocken State Road, Suite 500
West Conshohocken, PA 19428
www.templetonpress.org

Designed and typeset by Gopa & Ted2, Inc.

ISBN13: 978-1-59947-518-9
eISBN13: 978-1-59947-519-6

Library of Congress Cataloging-in-Publication Data on file.

Printed in the United States of America

17 18 19 20 21   10 9 8 7 6 5 4 3 2 1

Contents

———————— ≳≲ ————————

False Black Power?

Introduction

⊱⊰

IN 1976, HERBERT GUTMAN, a professor of history at the City College of New York, published *The Black Family in Slavery and Freedom, 1750–1925*. As Gutman explained in his introduction, the book was an extensive response to Daniel Patrick Moynihan's controversial 1965 government study on the black family. Moynihan, who at the time was an assistant secretary in President Lyndon Johnson's Labor Department, asserted in his report that the "the Negro family in urban ghettos is crumbling," as evidenced by the increase in single female-headed households. Recent civil rights gains notwithstanding, he observed, family composition still mattered, and the growing percentage of black children being raised in fatherless homes did not bode well for narrowing racial disparities in America between blacks and whites. Moynihan's warnings about the effects of family structure on black socioeconomic outcomes were dismissed by his detractors as victim-blaming bigotry, but rising rates of violent crime, welfare use, and other social problems among poor blacks in subsequent decades would ultimately vindicate the future New York senator.

Gutman's criticism, however, was of a different and more fundamental nature. The Moynihan report rooted this black family disorganization in slavery and Jim Crow, experiences that supposedly had undermined the position of men in poor black households and made matriarchal black families the norm. "It was by destroying the Negro family that white America broke the will of the Negro people," wrote Moynihan. This analysis essentially was a rehash of consensus scholarly thought at the time. The black sociologist E. Franklin Frazier, from whose writings Moynihan borrowed heavily, had made very similar arguments decades earlier in his 1939 study, *The Negro Family in the United States*. W. E. B. Du Bois and Kenneth Stampp were other prominent scholars who also had blamed white racism for the demise of two-parent black families. Nevertheless, Gutman argued that this popular thesis was deeply flawed, and his book set out to rebut it empirically.

"Our objective was simple," wrote Gutman, whose initial research was conducted with fellow historian Laurence Glasco. "If enslavement caused the widespread development among Afro-Americans of 'a fatherless matrifocal [mother-centered] family' sufficiently strong to be transmitted from generation to generation, thereby affecting the beliefs and behavior of descendants of eighteenth-century African slaves who lived in mid-twentieth-century northern urban ghettos, such a condition should have been even more common among urban Afro-Americans closer to the time of slavery."

Yet that's not what the evidence indicated. After reviewing Confederate plantation records, census forms in various cities and counties in the North and South, interviews with ex-slaves, and other material, Gutman and Glasco determined the following: during slavery, its immediate aftermath, and on through the first quarter of the twentieth century, the vast majority of black children were raised in two-parent households; black marriages were as long lasting and stable as the marriages of economically comparable whites; and the black female-headed homes that did exist tended to be, like their white counterparts, comprised of older widows, not teenagers raising children alone.

Gutman's study of the black community in Buffalo, New York, from the 1850s through the 1920s, for example, showed that the "double-headed kin related household always was the characteristic Buffalo Afro-American household, ranging from 82 percent to 92 percent." A broader examination of data on southern rural and urban black households only "confirmed the Buffalo study." Gutman's findings demonstrated that blacks living in big cities had similar cultural patterns. An examination of 13,924 black families in New York City in 1925 revealed that 85 percent were two-parent homes, more than 80 percent of children under age six lived with both parents, and fewer than 8 percent of the households surveyed featured "male-absent" families headed by women between twenty-five and forty-four years old.

Gutman's pioneering research offered empirical evidence

that the family structure and culture we see among poor blacks today is an outgrowth of something more recent than black bondage and legal segregation. The reality is that single parenting was rare among blacks in earlier times, even in the antebellum South. The social pathologies manifest in black ghetto communities after World War II were born of other factors, despite wide speculation that the institution of slavery was primarily to blame. Yet, more than four decades after the publication of *The Black Family in Slavery and Freedom*, Gutman's findings remain mostly ignored by scholars, elected officials, policymakers, and commentators who are invested in the notion that slavery and Jim Crow offer satisfactory explanations of dysfunctional black behavior in the twenty-first century. And with too few exceptions, social scientists cowed by political correctness are still downplaying or denying the strong connection between black poverty and black family structure.

In the pages that follow, I argue broadly that the current focus on white racism and political solutions to racial gaps continues to miss the mark. Our national discussions spend ample time on the impact of slavery but precious little on the black social and economic trends that followed the growth of the modern welfare state. In the postslavery era, the differences in black progress before and after the Great Society interventions are glaring. When intact families were commonplace, the rise in black education, incomes, and occupations was significant and steady. As black family disorganization intensified and wealth-transfer programs grew in size and scope, that progress slowed in some cases and stalled in others. Liberals have attempted to compensate for black cultural retrogression since the 1960s with increased black political power. In 2008, America elected her first black president, and eight years later, one undeniable lesson was that political clout is no substitute for self-development.

≷

I AM INDEBTED to Susan Arellano of Templeton Press, who initiated this book and helped in shaping the material. I also thank the Manhattan Institute, where I am a senior fellow and have the time and freedom to explore issues with the support of dedicated colleagues who are far more interested in finding truth than being popular. Finally, I am grateful to the Thomas W. Smith Foundation, the Searle Freedom Trust, and the Dian Graves Owen Foundation, whose generosity makes my work possible.

PART I

※

False Black Power

CHAPTER 1

The Civil Rights Distraction

≳≲

ONE DAY IN FALL 2002, I opened my newspaper to read that the Reverends Jesse Jackson and Al Sharpton were upset over some dialogue in the new hit movie *Barbershop*. The nation's most prominent civil rights activists had threatened to call for a boycott of the ensemble comedy unless the filmmakers agreed to issue a public apology and delete the offending material from future DVD versions.[1] I looked up from the paper and chuckled to myself. Perhaps there was something that could better recommend a film to me than Jackson and Sharpton not wanting me to see it, but nothing came to mind immediately. Not then and not now. I grabbed a jacket, headed to the theater, and caught the next showing. I laughed from beginning to end and left the multiplex with a renewed appreciation of the diminishing relevance of a civil rights old guard personified by the likes of Jackson and Sharpton.

The controversy turned out to be excellent publicity for a relatively low-budget film aimed primarily at black audiences. *Barbershop* was the top money-maker at the box office the weekend it was released. Written, produced, and directed by blacks, it's set on Chicago's crime-ridden South Side and features a nearly all-black cast. The story centers around Calvin, an exasperated young husband whose wife is expecting their first child and who dreams of opening his own music studio but is stuck running a barbershop he inherited from his father. The plot is predictable for the most part—Calvin, who's played by rapper-turned-actor Ice Cube, eventually comes to appreciate his inheritance—but nobody hails *Barbershop* because of the storyline. Rather, the film's main appeal is the dialogue: free-wheeling verbal exchanges that Calvin's esoteric crew of barbers—including old-timer Eddie and ex-con Ricky—have with one another and their customers. Topics cover not only sports and music and women, which you'd expect, but also topics like race relations and dating and urban crime. The sharp, edgy comedic riffs are often insightful and sometimes shock you with their bluntness.

The movie isn't overtly political but its social conservatism is unmistakable. Characters celebrate self-help and personal responsibility while refusing to be condescended to or pitied. The overriding ethos is that blacks can and should be advancing by dint of hard work, not white guilt, and it's largely their own fault if they aren't. "Black people in this country are some of the richest negroes on the planet," says Ricky to a young black man who blames his inability to find a job on racism. "Everywhere you look, there's opportunity." After

THE CIVIL RIGHTS DISTRACTION   13

one customer, a dim-witted small-time crook, announces that ancestral slavery has "ruined my whole life," and another suggests that blacks demand reparations from the government to improve their lot, Eddie interjects that blacks already receive government compensation for slavery in the form of welfare payments and affirmative action. Ricky takes the antireparations argument even further and insists that today's black ghetto culture is the more significant impediment to group success. "We don't need reparations. We need restraint," he explains. "Don't go out and buy a Range Rover when you livin' with your momma. And pay your momma some rent." Ricky isn't finished. "Can we please, please try to teach our kids something other than [rap music] . . . and please, black people, be on time for something other than free [admission] before 11 at the club."

In the film, Ricky's listeners nod in approval and applaud. So too, I noticed, did several other black people sitting nearby in my Brooklyn theater. I was stunned by the exchange. It wasn't the sentiments expressed—those are commonplace among everyday blacks, if not among their self-appointed spokespeople. The surprise was to hear them being voiced by black protagonists in a mainstream Hollywood film, which was much less common. Here was a work of fiction that required no suspension of my disbelief. I readily recognized this place. My father took me to this barbershop on Buffalo's struggling east side as a boy.[2] It's the clip shop I frequented—when I still had hair—on Flatbush Avenue in Brooklyn after moving to New York City in my twenties. It's where black people from all backgrounds—the college grad and the high-school dropout, the businessman and the bus driver—gather and make observations that are as raw and heartfelt as they are politically incorrect. Two minutes of film dialogue had produced a more honest conversation about race than ten-thousand-word magazine essays by Ta-Nehisi Coates and Michael Eric Dyson or a dozen panel discussions on CNN, where talking heads dance around uncomfortable truths, and expressing Ricky and Eddie's views about the black under-class might get you escorted from the premises by build-ing security. In this sense, the entire movie's message is an affront to black leaders like Al Sharpton and Jesse Jackson as well as the liberal intellectuals who trade on the notion that black America is all but helpless in the face of an oppressive white society. The can-do attitudes on display undermine the agenda of a black political elite that benefits from portraying underprivileged minorities as perpetual victims in need of more government remedies.

The scenes that set off the reverends—and which, thank-fully, remained in the DVD version—are surprisingly innoc-uous given all the fuss they generated. The cantankerous Eddie, who's played by comedian Cedric the Entertainer, pokes fun at Martin Luther King Jr.'s philandering and down-plays Rosa Parks's famous act of disobedience in Montgom-ery, Alabama, in 1955 by pointing out that she was far from the first black person to refuse to give up a seat on the bus.

In the same scene, Eddie also insists that O. J. Simpson "did it" and that black motorist Rodney King had it coming for resisting arrest. When an appalled customer warns Eddie that Jesse Jackson better not hear him talking like that, Eddie responds, "Fuck Jesse Jackson!" Eddie's irreverence produces some of the movie's biggest laughs.

The veracity of Eddie's remarks isn't really the issue. There's not much doubt that King strayed, according to his contemporaries and biographers.[3] And what really distinguished Parks, as Eddie explains, were her ties to the National Association for the Advancement of Colored People (NAACP), not her willingness to ignore a racist law. At least three other blacks in Montgomery alone had been arrested earlier in 1955 for defiant behavior similar to Parks's.[4] It's also worth noting that in neither scene do Eddie's rants go over well with onlookers, who either challenge him or howl in disapproval of his outlandishly disrespectful tone. Nevertheless, Sharpton compared the film to the FBI's efforts to discredit Dr. King in the 1960s and even took offense at the Rodney King crack.[5] Jackson insisted that he was unbothered by the attacks on himself and was merely defending the film's other targets because they couldn't defend themselves. "The filmmakers crossed the line between what's sacred and serious and what's funny," he said at the time. "I could dismiss the comments about me, but Dr. King is dead and Ms. Parks is an invalid."[6] Maybe so, but even fellow liberals thought Sharpton and Jackson's objections were silly and unnecessary.

Typical was the response from *Washington Post* columnist Donna Britt, who questioned the "logic that tells Jackson and Sharpton that jokes in the movie 'Barbershop' merit public complaint and censure. All because the No. 1 comedy, which celebrates an inner-city barbershop, does what black, white, brown and yellow Americans do in real life every day: Poke fun at folks whom we admire." Indeed, a photo of Jackson, a Chicago resident, is displayed on the wall of the barbershop in the movie. Britt added that "it takes nerve, assuming your displeasure is shared by millions and implying that some offhand lines in a sweet movie can smear a dead hero or defenseless invalid." When she asked a friend why Jackson was wasting his time on an issue like this, the response was, "Because it's his job."[7] That friend sounds like Eddie.

Fifty years ago, Jesse Jackson's job was fighting Jim Crow. Today his job is to maintain his own relevance long after America's civil rights battles have been fought successfully. To stay relevant, Jackson, Sharpton, the NAACP, and the civil rights establishment prefer to present black Americans as an aggrieved group whose problems stem mainly from the actions of others. And they insist that black advancement is contingent on direct-action protests and political solutions. It's no wonder that the country's most prominent civil rights activists had little use for a film that depicts black men discussing what they could and should be doing for themselves instead of what others should be doing for them.

The popularity of *Barbershop* led to two sequels, both of

which continue the barbed social commentary of the first film. *Barbershop 2: Back in Business*, released two years after the original, includes several scenes that flash back to the 1960s. In one, Black Panthers are parodied as suicidal socio-paths, while another shows Calvin's father and a young Eddie protecting the barbershop during the 1968 Chicago riots that followed Dr. King's assassination. "This ain't right," says the father while staring out of his shop's front window at black looters setting ablaze cars and businesses. "We should be honoring the man's memory. We shouldn't be doing this." The movie also features a crooked black politician named Lalowe Brown, whom Eddie derisively refers to as "Lalowe Sharpton"—perhaps in a bit of payback for Al Sharpton's previous boycott threats.

The third installment of the series, *Barbershop: The Next Cut*, landed in theaters in 2016, the final year of Barack Obama's presidency. The movie introduces several new characters, including a black barber named Rashad, who has a teenage son with discipline problems, and an Indian American barber named Raja, who says things like, "Maybe we need to stop waiting for the government to step in and save us and we need to start saving ourselves." In addition to debating Obama's legacy, characters discuss fatherhood, child-rearing, sexism—the barbershop now doubles as a beauty salon—urban violence, and high-profile shootings of black males.

Like the previous films, we get a humorous glimpse at what

blacks sometimes discuss—and how they discuss it—when whites aren't around. We also get a realistic presentation of a cross section of black thinking on hot-button issues. Diverse black viewpoints aren't regularly represented in mainstream news outlets, where the politically liberal view is presumed to be the black view, and the opinions of more conservative blacks are downplayed or ignored altogether.

In the third film, the clip shop now has a "No Guns Allowed" sign on the wall, and the main plot centers on efforts to reduce the city's epidemic of black-on-black crime—a storyline that once again requires no suspension of disbelief. In 2016, Chicago recorded more than 4,300 shootings and its highest murder rate in two decades.[8] The overwhelming majority of shooting victims were black, and more than 99 percent of the shootings were carried out by civilians, not the police. Protest groups want us to focus on the behavior of law enforcement, and the media too often does that, but it's obvious that young black men in places like Chicago live in fear of being gunned down by other young black men, not by cops. "It's not up to me to decide what activists should protest, but after years of dealing with the realities of street violence, I don't understand how a movement called 'Black Lives Matter' can ignore the leading cause of death among young black men in the U.S., which is homicide by their peers," wrote a retired New York City police detective in 2015. "Since 2001, even as rates of violent crime have dropped dramatically, more than 90,000 black men in the U.S. have been killed by other black men. With fatalities on this scale, the term epidemic is not a metaphor. Every year, the casualty count of black-on-black crime is twice that of the death toll of 9/11."[9]

Nationwide, crime has fallen on average from where it was in the early 1990s, but in recent years violent crime is up on average in the most populated cities.[10] And whichever way crime is trending, low-income minorities still bear the brunt of it. In a 2016 Gallup poll, 53 percent of all respondents said that they worry "a great deal" about crime and violence, which was up from 39 percent two years earlier and at a fifteen-year high. Moreover, respondents who were low income and nonwhite expressed by far the most anxiety, which makes sense given that they are by far the most likely crime victims. "More broadly, those with no college education are roughly twice as likely as those with a college degree to worry about crime," reported Gallup, "and those living in households earning less than $30,000 per year are much more likely than those earning at least $75,000 to worry about crime and violence. Nonwhites' concern about crime is much higher than whites' worry about the issue."[11]

An early scene in *Next Cut* has several characters one-upping each other with stories about being robbed and assaulted in the neighborhood. After a barber remarks that he was robbed twice in one day on the same block, his customer scoffs, "That ain't shit. Last week, I got robbed twice—*and* got my ass beat by the second robber for giving all my money to the first."

Foes of "mass incarceration" of black men seem much more concerned with the plight of criminals than with the plight of the most likely crime victims. As president, Obama shortened the sentences of over one thousand federal inmates, which was more than the previous eleven presidents combined.[12] On the campaign trail in 2016, Hillary Clinton railed against "excessive" incarceration, but if you live in a community with excessive crime and violence, you might see things differently. The former first family lives in a predominantly white New York City suburb where multimillion dollar homes are commonplace and where violent crime is as rare as black residents. The people she is so reluctant to lock up and so eager to cut slack aren't terrorizing her neighborhood.

In *Next Cut*, Calvin and his wife now have a fourteen-year-old son, Jalen, whom they are desperately trying to shield from South Side Chicago's dangerous gang culture. Like its predecessors, the movie heartedly embraces what liberals derisively refer to as "respectability politics," or the assumption that a person's behavior and presentation play an important role in getting ahead. One conversation between Calvin and his son goes as follows:

CALVIN: Tomorrow, I'm going to reintroduce you to the concept of a belt. Ain't nobody want to see your butt cheeks.

JALEN: Nobody wears no belts. They corny.

CALVIN: Yeah. Well, so is getting shot.

Or take another exchange, between Calvin and Rashad, on the need for black people to take responsibility for their circumstances, not shift blame or look to political saviors:

> CALVIN: I'm so tired of this mess. Every time I turn around somebody killing somebody over nothing. What are we supposed to do? Lock our doors, don't snitch, pretend like this shit is normal? . . . It's not normal.

> RASHAD: Then we got to do something about it. Shorties [kids] out here wilding, and that's our fault. That's on us. If we don't do something, no one's going to save our community. We gotta take our streets back.

Some of the most interesting discussions in the movie concern the impact of Obama's presidency on the condition of everyday blacks. After Raja cites Obama's election as a sign of racial progress, Rashad pushes back. "What does that mean for the average black dude walking down the street?" he asks before citing the names of black shooting victims who have made national headlines in recent years, such as Trayvon Martin, Michael Brown, and Freddie Gray. "A madman walked into a Charleston church and killed nine innocent people. Did [Obama's] blackness stop that?" asks Rashad. It's a passionate speech, but the filmmakers chose to give Raja the last word in the exchange, and he urges Rashad to put things in perspective. "I'm not saying that stuff isn't messed up because it is," says Raja. "What I'm saying is that there's never been a better time to be a black person in this country than right now."

Raja is right. Blacks today are more likely to experience group preferences than racial sleights, and they have legal recourse when discrimination does occur. In the 1960s, black people risked life and limb to cast a ballot. In 2012, black voter turnout exceeded white turnout.[13] Moreover, white attitudes toward blacks have changed tremendously over the decades. The scholars Stephan and Abigail Thernstrom noted that in 1944, just 42 percent of whites opposed racial discrimination in employment, but by 1963 some 83 percent did. And that was just one of several indications that racial attitudes were shifting rapidly and well before the landmark Civil Rights Act of 1964 and Voting Rights Act of 1965 had passed. The Thernstroms continued:

Similarly, support for school integration jumped from 30 to 62 percent between 1942 and 1963, for integrated public transportation from 44 to 79 percent, and for neighborhood integration from 35 to 64 percent. It has sometimes been suggested that fed-

eral civil rights legislation in the 1960s was responsible for the huge shift in white racial attitudes, but
that puts the cart before the horse. Deep attitudinal
changes created the political pressures responsible
for the enactment of new law.[14]

More recently, black politicians such as US Representa-
tives Emanuel Cleaver of Missouri, Keith Ellison of Minne-
sota, and Mia Love of Utah were elected to Congress from
districts that are more than 60 percent white. South Carolina,
a state where whites are over 68 percent of the population,
has elected an Asian American governor and a black US senator. Racism has by no means been vanquished from America,
but the problems that blacks face today are different from
the problems they faced in the past. In twenty-first-century
America, employers are eager to hire black workers, and
schools compete to admit black students. Racial attitudes
have evolved to the point where a black man in a country
that is only 13 percent black was twice elected president and
ended his second term with a personal approval rating of
nearly 60 percent. The major barrier to black progress today
is not racial discrimination and hasn't been for decades.
The challenge for blacks is to better position themselves to
take advantage of existing opportunities, and that involves
addressing the antisocial, self-defeating behaviors and habits
and attitudes endemic to the black underclass.

≳≲

Politicians and activists aren't the only ones who prefer to minimize black personal responsibility when discussing racial disparities. Academics and commentators who intellectualize and justify black social pathology are also culpable. Ideology often trumps common sense, and behavior that ought to be repudiated is romanticized and even praised as representative of black authenticity. Empirical data that undermines faddish thinking gets ignored altogether or subordinated to a more politically correct analysis of racial inequality. In a *New York Times* op-ed, sociologist Orlando Patterson chided his fellow social scientists for their reluctance to even consider how certain cultural traits impact black outcomes. "The main cause for this shortcoming," wrote Patterson, "is a deep-seated dogma that has prevailed in social science and policy circles since the mid-1960s: the rejection of any explanation that invokes a group's cultural attributes—its distinctive attitudes, values and predispositions, and the resulting behavior of its members—and the relentless preference for relying on structural factors like low incomes, joblessness, poor schools and bad housing."[15] Elsewhere, Patterson argued that those structural factors shouldn't be ignored, but neither should cultural factors. Yet for "decades, there was hostility, approaching derision, to any cultural study of the poor, including black youth," he wrote. "While it has become legitimate again to probe the cultural life of the disadvantaged, social scientists continue to tread warily, and one kind of cultural analysis remains suspect: attempts to explain social problems in cultural terms."[16]

The sociologist William Julius Wilson agreed with Patterson that any serious consideration of black cultural handicaps remains largely taboo. "Many liberal scholars are reluctant to discuss or research the role that culture plays in the negative outcomes found in the inner city," he writes. Wilson speculates that social scientists might "fear being criticized for reinforcing the popular view that negative social outcomes—poverty, unemployment, drug addiction, crime—are due to the shortcomings of the people themselves."[17] The fear is plausible, unfortunately. The harsh reaction to Daniel Patrick Moynihan's 1965 study of the black family, which highlighted troubling cultural trends among inner-city blacks, still resonates in academia. "Moynihan argued that growing up in homes without a male breadwinner reduced black children's chances of climbing out of poverty, and that the spread of such families would make it hard for blacks to take advantage of the legal and institutional changes flowing from the civil rights revolution," explained sociologists Sara McLanahan and Christopher Jencks. "Moynihan's claim that growing up in a fatherless family reduced a child's chances of educational and economic success was furiously denounced when the report appeared in 1965, with many critics calling

Moynihan a racist. For the next two decades, few scholars chose to investigate the effects of father absence, lest they too be demonized if their findings supported Moynihan's argument."[18]

In other words, the same liberals who profess such a deep concern for the plight of the black underclass have for decades refused to honestly assess the role of ghetto culture in black outcomes out of fear of where the facts might lead. Journalists, academics, policymakers, and civil rights leaders have shown minimal interest in examining the trends that Moynihan identified, even as the evidence in his favor mounted. In the mid-1960s, about 25 percent of black children and 5 percent of white children lived in a household headed by a single mother. Over the next two decades, the black percentage doubled and the racial gap widened, even as blacks gained political clout and Great Society programs and other measures directed massive amounts of resources at the urban poor.[19]

It's instructive to compare trends in black America in the decades preceding and following these welfare state interventions, though liberals have little interest in doing so because such comparisons undermine the notion that white racism is the primary culprit in black-white disparities today. However, census data shows black marriage rates exceeding white rates in the first half of the twentieth century.[20] Prior to the early 1960s, black arrest rates were falling, and the homicide rate for black males was declining at a faster rate than the overall homicide rate. In the 1950s, the black homicide rate fell by 22 percent for black males while remaining essentially flat for white males. "It was a large reduction for a single decade," wrote Charles Murray. "It was all the more remarkable when one considers that it coincided with a period of rapid black migration into urban centers" where murder rates tend to be high. Following the government interventions of the 1960s, however, homicide rates climbed overall, and most sharply for black men. "Put simply, it was much more dangerous to be black in 1972 than it was in 1965, whereas it was not much more dangerous to be white."[21]

The family breakdown, social pathology, and economic blight seen today in places like Chicago, Detroit, Baltimore, Washington, and other cities with large black populations is commonly blamed on slavery and Jim Crow. But the available evidence belies that narrative and suggests that well-intentioned but misguided social policies of the 1960s better explain the circumstances of today's black underclass.

"Despite a high rate of poverty in ghetto neighborhoods throughout the first half of the twentieth century," wrote William Julius Wilson in the opening pages of his 1987 book, *The Truly Disadvantaged*, "rates of inner-city joblessness, teenage pregnancy, out-of-wedlock births, female-headed families, welfare dependency, and serious crime were significantly lower than in later years and did not reach catastrophic proportions until the mid-1970s." Elaborating, Wilson described Harlem and other poor black neighborhoods in the 1940s and 1950s:

> There was crime, to be sure, but it had not reached the point where people were fearful of walking the streets at night, despite the overwhelming poverty in the area. There was joblessness, but it was nowhere near the proportions of unemployment and labor-force nonparticipation that have gripped ghetto communities since 1970. There were single-parent families, but they were a small minority of all black families and tended to be incorporated within extended family networks and to be headed not by unwed teenagers and young adult women but by middle-aged women who usually were widowed, separated, or divorced. There were welfare recipients, but only a very small percentage of families could be said to be welfare-dependent. In short, unlike the present period, inner-city communities prior to 1960 exhibited the features of social organization—including a sense of community, positive neighborhood identification, and explicit norms and sanctions against aberrant behavior.[22]

Blacks living under Jim Crow conditions and only a couple generations out of bondage had more stable families and lived in safer communities than their counterparts living under a twice-elected black president. Seventy years ago, racial disparities in employment, educational attainment, poverty, crime, and income were narrowing, yet those trends would slow, stall, and, in some cases, reverse course in the wake of 1960s policy interventions and increasing black political power. For various reasons, liberals want to deny this historical reality or cast aspersions at anyone interested in exploring it. Shielding blacks from any responsibility for their situation today may seem kind in light of the atrocities that blacks have endured in the United States over the centuries, but the relevant question is whether it's helpful. More than anything else, the black underclass needs the human capital—values, habits, attitudes, behaviors—that has facilitated the economic advancement of other racial and ethnic groups and that indeed was facilitating unprecedented black advancement prior to the Great Society.

CHAPTER 2

The Limits of Politics

≥≤

P RESIDENT BARACK OBAMA traveled to Alabama on
March 7, 2015, to deliver a speech marking the fiftieth
anniversary of "Bloody Sunday," when six hundred peaceful
protesters seeking the right to vote were beaten and tear-
gassed by mounted police as they tried to march across Selma's Edmund Pettus Bridge. It was one of the more symbolic
moments of a deeply symbolic presidency—an opportunity
to remind the county of how much racial progress had been
made over the past half century. But Obama was interested
in more than just commemorating a turning point in the
civil rights struggles of the mid-twentieth century. And so a
speech rightly honoring "the courage of ordinary Americans
willing to endure billy clubs and the chastening rod" and
"keep marching toward justice" was laced with Democratic
talking points and comparisons between the problems that
blacks faced during legal discrimination and the problems
they faced five decades later. To that end, Obama's remarks
invoked "unfair sentencing" and "overcrowded prisons"
in the criminal justice system while making no mention of

black-white disparities in crime rates.[1] He also suggested that voter identification laws threaten the black franchise and suppress turnout. Yet in 2012, blacks voted at higher rates than whites, including in states with the most stringent voter identification mandates. And in 2014, voter turnout among all groups was slightly higher in Texas, which has a strict voter identification law, than it was in New York, which does not.[2]

Parallels between America under Jim Crow and America under a twice-elected black president and two black attorneys general may be tortured, but Obama also knew that such rhetoric plays well politically for the left and distracts from liberalism's poor track record in helping the black underclass. The goal is to keep black voters angry, paranoid, and content to put the onus on others to address racial disparities and negative black outcomes. The identity politics practiced by liberals today treats blacks not as individuals with agency but rather as a group of victims who are both blameless and helpless. "Liberalism in the twenty-first century is, for the most part, a moral manipulation that exaggerates inequity and unfairness in American life in order to justify overreaching public policies and programs," explained the author Shelby Steele. This liberalism is "invested in an overstatement of America's present sinfulness based on the nation's past sins. It conflates the past into the present so that the present is indistinguishable from the ugly past. And so modern liberalism is grounded in a paradox: it tries to be progressive and forward looking by fixing its gaze backward. It insists that America's shameful past is the best explanation of its current social problems."[3]

This liberal conflation of the past and present is without a doubt politically expedient—note how Democrats regularly dismiss any Republican criticism of liberal social policies as being motivated by racial hostility toward blacks—but it's hard to see how diverting attention from far more credible explanations of racial gaps today helps blacks advance. "Despite frequent assertions to the contrary, many of the seemingly intractable problems encountered by a significant number of black Americans do not result from racial discrimination," wrote economist Walter Williams in *Race and Economics: How Much Can Be Blamed on Discrimination?* "That is not to say discrimination does not exist. Nor is it to say discrimination has no adverse effects. For policy purposes, however, the issue is not whether or not racial discrimination exists but the extent to which it explains what we see today." The political left wins votes by telling black people that racism, in one form or another, explains racial disparities that only government programs can address. And groups like the NAACP raise money and stay relevant by pushing the same narrative—a narrative that also maintains broad and largely unquestioned support in the mainstream media.

A few days after Obama's Selma address, National Public Radio aired an interview with the city's mayor, George Evans. The interviewer wanted to know how "what happened in

Selma fifty years ago fits into the current conversation about race relations in this country." But Evans, the city's second black mayor, didn't see a clear connection between the problems that blacks faced five decades ago and current obstacles.

"I'm not sure how it fits," Evans responded. "We have a lot more crime going on in 2015 all over the country than we had in 1965. Segregation existed, but we didn't have the crime. So now, even though we've gained so much through voting rights and Bloody Sunday, we've stepped backwards when it comes to crime and drugs and the jail system—things like that."

Apparently, that wasn't the answer the interviewer was looking for, and so she pressed the mayor. "What's life like for the average citizen in Selma," where 80 percent of residents are black, she asked. "I mean, your city does have challenges. You've got chronic unemployment rates. What are the biggest problems from your vantage point?" Still, the mayor refused to do what Obama had done in his speech and make facile historical parallels.

"Well, from the standpoint of jobs, we have a lot of jobs," said Evans. "It's just that there are a lot of people who do not have the skill level to man these jobs. And that's the biggest problem we have. There are industries and businesses here that are searching for people to come to work. But many times they're not able to get the jobs because they're not going back to pick up that trade or that technical skill that's needed in order to take that job."[4]

The mayor may not have been telling National Public Radio what it wanted to hear, but his responses were perfectly sensible. After having declined significantly in the 1950s, including among blacks, violent crime began surging in the late 1960s. Although it has fallen since the early 1990s, the violent crime rate in 2014 was higher than it was in 1965 and has since returned to 1990s levels in major cities.[5] Evans's observation that a high unemployment rate can result from factors other than a shortage of jobs also jibes with the social science research. Moreover, sometimes the problem isn't a lack of jobs or even job skills so much as a lack of interest in filling the jobs that are available. The 2015 Baltimore riots that followed the death of a black suspect in police custody were linked by some observers to high unemployment rates in the ghetto.[6] But a black construction worker at a job site that had been looted told a reporter that in his experience the neighborhood youths who were "protesting" seemed to have little interest in finding legitimate employment. "I see about 30 people walking by here every day, and only about two of them will bother to ask whether we're hiring," he said. "You have some brilliant kids, extraordinary talent, but they don't see opportunity."[7]

The evidence that factors other than a lack of job opportunities may contribute significantly to high black unemployment rates dates back decades and is more than anecdotal. In 1986, the National Bureau of Economic Research released a detailed study of poor communities in Boston, Philadelphia, and Chicago. It found that almost half (46 percent) of black youths who were not in school and not working said it was "very easy" or "somewhat easy" to find a job working as a laborer, and 71 percent said the same of landing a minimum-wage job.[8] The researchers also reported that "the typical out-of-school, nonemployed" black youth in the ghetto wasn't especially focused on enhancing his or her employment prospects. Instead, "the youths reported spending most of their time on 'hanging out,' 'TV/ movies,' 'listening to music,' or 'getting high,' as opposed to searching for jobs, reading, or working around the house."[9]

Harvard economist Richard Freeman, one of the study's authors, wrote that an "important alternative to work for youths in general, and for black youths in particular, is crime." Nearly a third of the youths (32 percent) said they could earn more from criminal activity than from legitimate work, and those "who committed crimes, who used drugs or drank, who saw crime as a relatively lucrative option to work and who perceived the risk and the penalties of being caught as modest, had markedly lower chances of being in school or of holding a job." He added that as "a policy matter, these other social problems must also be addressed in any major effort to resolve the black youth employment problem."[10]

Yet the report also noted that much of the social policy aimed at helping this subgroup wasn't having the intended effect:

One of the more depressing results of the study is our finding that youths whose families received assistance from major public programs for disadvantaged families did worse in the job market. Youths from welfare homes with the same family income and otherwise comparable to youths from non-welfare homes had a much worse experience in the job market. If there were a natural reduction of the number of families on welfare, the odds are that the youths would benefit as well as the rest of their families. Youths living in public housing projects also did less well than youths living in private housing.[11]

≥≤

Since the 1960s, black leaders have placed a heavy emphasis on seeking political power. The assumption—rarely challenged—is that black political clout is a prerequisite of black socioeconomic advancement. It's true that passage of the Voting Rights Act of 1965 was followed by large increases in black elected officials. In the Deep South, black officeholders grew from 100 in 1964 to 4,300 in 1978. By the early 1980s, major US cities with large black populations, such as Cleveland, Detroit, Chicago, Washington, and Philadelphia, had elected black mayors. Between 1970 and 2010, the number of black elected officials nationwide increased from fewer than fifteen hundred to more than ten thousand. Yet the socioeconomic progress that was supposed to follow in the wake of these political gains never materialized. During an era of growing black political influence and the expansion of social programs such as racial preferences, blacks as a group progressed at a slower rate than whites, and the black poor actually lost ground.

In a 1991 book, social scientist Gary Orfield and his coauthor, journalist Carole Ashkinaze, assessed the progress of blacks in the 1970s and 1980s following the sharp increase in black officeholders. The thinking, then and now, was that the problems of the cities "were basically the result of the racism of white officials and that many could be solved by black mayors, school superintendents, policemen and teachers who were displacing white ones." The expectation, they added, "was that black political and education leaders would be able to make large moves toward racial equity simply by devising policies and practices reflecting their understanding of the background and needs of black people."[12] But the integration of these institutions proved to be insufficient. "Many blacks have reached positions of local power, such as mayor, county commission chairman or superintendent of schools, positions undreamed of 30 years ago," they wrote. Their findings, however, showed that "these achievements do not necessarily produce success for blacks as a whole."[13] The empirical evidence, they said, "indicates that there may be little relationship between the success of local black leaders and the opportunities of typical black families."[14]

When Michael Brown was shot dead after assaulting a police officer in Ferguson, Missouri, in 2014, a large fuss was made over the racial composition of the police department and city leaders, which supposedly explained the subsequent unrest. A Justice Department report responding to the incident noted that although the city's population was 67 percent black, just four of its fifty-four police officers fit that description. "While a diverse police department does not guarantee a constitutional one, it is nonetheless critically important for law enforcement agencies, and the Ferguson Police Department in particular, to strive for broad diversity among officers and civilian staff," said the Justice Department.[15] But if racial diversity among law enforcement and city officials is so "critically important," what explains the rioting in Baltimore the following year after a black suspect there died in police custody? At the time, 63 percent of Baltimore's residents and 40 percent of its police officers were black. The Baltimore police commissioner also was black, along with the mayor and a majority of the city council. Contentious relations between the police and ghetto communities are driven mainly by high crime rates in those areas, something that the political left doesn't like to acknowledge. The sharp rise in violent crime in our inner cities coincides with the increase of black leaders in many of those very same cities, which makes it hard to argue that racist or indifferent authorities are to blame. What can be said of Baltimore is also true of Cleveland, Detroit, Philadelphia, Atlanta, New

Orleans, and Washington, DC, where black mayors, police chiefs, city council members, and school superintendents have held sway for decades.

In her 1995 book, *Facing Up to the American Dream*, political scientist Jennifer Hochschild examined data from the late 1950s to the early 1990s—an era the covers not only growing black political clout but also the implementation of the War on Poverty and two full decades of affirmative action policies in hiring and college admissions. Hochschild reported that between 1959 and 1992, poverty fell from 55 percent to 33 percent for blacks and from 18 percent to 12 percent for whites, which meant that the "ratio of black to white poverty has remained at 3—hardly a victory in the war on racially disproportionate poverty." The absolute numbers, she added, "tell the same story: there are now about four million fewer poor whites than thirty years ago, but 686,000 *more* poor blacks." Moreover, low-income blacks lost ground to low-income whites over the same period. Between 1967 and 1992, incomes for the poorest fifth of blacks declined at more than double the rate of comparable whites.[16]

≥≤

This history should have served to temper expectations for the first black president. Without taking away anything from Obama's historic accomplishment, or the country's widespread sense of pride in the racial progress that his election symbolized, the reality is that there was little reason to believe that a black president was the answer to racial inequities or the problems of the black poor. Most groups in America and elsewhere who have risen economically have done so with little or no political influence, and groups that have enjoyed early political success have tended to rise more slowly. "Group cohesion, expressed in political pressure and bloc voting, is often regarded as axiomatically the most effective method of promoting group progress," explained Thomas Sowell. But historically, "the relationship between political success and economic success has been more nearly inverse than direct."[17] Germans, Jews, Italians, and Asians are among those who saw economic gains precede political gains in America. Similarly, the ethnic Chinese in Southeast Asia, the English and Italians in Argentina, and Jews in Britain, among many other examples, all prospered economically while mostly shunning politics. "Empirically, political activity and political success have been neither necessary nor sufficient for economic advancement," explained Sowell. "Nor has eager political participation or outstanding success in politics been translated into faster group achievement."[18]

A counterexample is the Irish, whose rise from poverty was especially slow even though Irish-run political organizations in places like Boston and Philadelphia dominated local government. The Irish had more political success than any other ethnic group historically, according to Sowell. "Yet the Irish were the slowest rising of all European immigrants to America. The wealth and power of a relatively few Irish political bosses had little impact on the progress of masses of Irish Americans."[19]

Even if a group has the ability to wield political influence, they don't always choose to do so. German immigrants to the United States in colonial times were not lacking in numbers. In Pennsylvania, they were one-third of the population, a situation that was not lost on non-Germans. "Why should Pennsylvania, founded by the English, become a colony of aliens, who will shortly become so numerous as to Germanize us instead of us Anglifying them?" wrote Benjamin Franklin in 1751. Nevertheless, Germans, many of whom arrived as indentured servants and focused on paying off the cost of their voyage, had other priorities and were well-known for avoiding politics. Germans began entering politics only after they had already risen economically.

Viewed against this history, many blacks were expecting Obama's presidency to deliver more prosperity than political clout tends to deliver for a group—in the United States or anywhere else. The black experience in America is of course different from the Irish experience, which in turn is different from the Chinese or German or Jewish experience. Indeed, we can't even generalize about all blacks in the United States, since the experience of black natives is different from the experience of black immigrants from the Caribbean and Africa. But that doesn't mean group cultural traits that show patterns of success or failure should be ignored. Even if we can't make perfect apples-to-apples comparisons, it doesn't mean we can't make any comparisons or draw any conclusions. Many different racial and ethnic minority groups have experienced various degrees of hardship in the United States and in other countries all over the world. How those groups have dealt with those circumstances is something to study closely and draw lessons from going forward—even if the only lesson is to manage expectations. As Sowell documented, we know from the experiences of Jews in Europe, the English and Italians in Argentina, and the ethnic Chinese minority in countries throughout Southeast Asia that being despised or denied equal rights or even having wealth confiscated by governments cannot stop a minority group from prospering economically if it has developed the necessary skills and habits and values. We know that black Americans in the first half of the twentieth century—during the darkest decades of Jim Crow, when racial discrimination was widespread, legal, and often ruthlessly enforced—nevertheless managed to climb out of poverty and gain access to white-collar professions at unprecedented rates that have never since been replicated, even after the passage of landmark civil rights legislation in the 1960s and the implementation of affirmative action programs in the 1970s.

One of the clear lessons from this history is that human capital has proven to be far more important than political capital in getting ahead. And that reality helps to explain why blacks fared the way they did not only in the Obama era but also in the preceding decades. Obama's election was the culmination of a civil rights strategy that prioritized political power to advance blacks, and eight years later we once again learned the limitations of that strategy. Orfield and Ashkinaze, who focused on black progress in Atlanta, a city that had long been run by black officials, found that black politicians behaved like their white counterparts and placed their own political survival above the needs of the underclass. "Black officials, like their white predecessors, tend to publicize successes, not problems," they wrote. "Moreover, while it was considered anti-black to ignore institutional failings when these institutions were headed by whites, some now see it as anti-black to call attention to failings in institutions headed by blacks. Today, black-controlled bureaucracies may hesitate to disclose vital information about damage caused by federal and state policy rather than risk being blamed for the results." Black officials were also treated differently by the media and in ways that didn't necessary help the black electorate hold them accountable. The authors speculated that the "dominant white media" fear "charges of racism by black administrators if they are too critical," and cited as an example the fact that "the press uncritically reported extremely misleading test scores from the overwhelmingly black Atlanta public schools for years until the state government forced the release of accurate data."[20]

A more recent example is the 2015 conviction of 11

Atlanta public school educators for their roles in what prosecutors described as one of the largest test-cheating scandals in US history. An earlier state investigation implicated 178 teachers and administrators in 44 mostly low-income Atlanta public schools. More than 80 of the accused confessed to tampering with exams. All 11 of those convicted were black. The alleged ringleader, a black former school superintendent, was indicted and faced forty-five years in prison if convicted but died of cancer before her trial was completed.[21]

Barack Obama's presidency provides more evidence that black prosperity will not flow naturally from black political influence. When Obama took office in 2009, the jobless rate was 12.7 percent for blacks and 7.1 percent for whites. At the start of his second term, in January 2013, the jobless rate had grown to 13.7 percent for blacks but remained unchanged for whites, which means that the black-white unemployment gap under Obama didn't just continue but also got wider. By November 2014, black unemployment had ticked down to 11 percent, but it was still more than double the white rate of 4.9 percent.[22]

Blacks did not see their average unemployment rate fall below double-digits until March 2015, the third month of Obama's seventh year in office.[23] The employment situation for blacks and other groups continued to improve in the final year of the Obama administration, but as late as June 2016 the black unemployment rate of 8.6 percent remained significantly worse than the rate for Hispanics (5.8 percent), whites

(4.4 percent), and Asians (3.5 percent). And the unemployment rate for blacks in states with large black populations—including Michigan, Illinois, Pennsylvania, Ohio, Alabama, and Louisiana—was well above the black national average.[24] The black unemployment rate had fallen to a relatively low 7.8 percent for blacks in December 2016, Obama's last month in office, but that doesn't reflect how a black electorate that consistently gave the president his highest marks had fared in the labor market for almost all of the Obama era.[25]

Because the official unemployment rate only captures the share of people who are actively seeking work and ignores those who have given up looking, it offers an incomplete and sometimes misleading measure of the economy. A lower unemployment rate can mean that more people are finding work, or it can mean that fewer people are searching for a job. That's why economists also want to know the labor force participation rate, which measures the share of the working-age population that's either employed or actively searching for work. And even if you discount Obama's first year in office, when his policies had yet to be fully implemented or take effect, labor force participation during his presidency was dismal. Growth in the labor force "slowed dramatically to less than half the rate of the previous four presidencies," wrote Daniel Griswold of George Mason University. Declining labor force participation did not begin under Obama but it did accelerate on his watch, especially for blacks. In December 2013, black labor force participation was 60.3

percent, a thirty-two-year low. For the country as a whole, labor force participation fell from 65.7 percent in January 2009 to 62.7 percent in December 2016, the worst rate since 1978.[26] For blacks, it fell from 63.2 percent to 61.8 percent over the same period.[27]

Poverty is another area where black outcomes during the Obama years were mediocre at best. During his first term, poverty rose among whites, from 9.4 percent in 2009 to 9.7 percent in 2012, a 3.2 percent increase, but it rose among blacks more significantly, from 25.8 percent to 27.2 percent, a 5.4 percent increase.[28] By 2015, the black poverty rate was down to 24.1 percent, but that was still more than two and a half times the 9.1 percent poverty rate among whites.[29] Racial gaps in homeownership and income also increased during the Obama presidency. In 2009, the homeownership rate for blacks was 46 percent and would fall to 42 percent in 2016. Whites also saw a decline in homeownership but it was much less severe—from 72 percent to 71 percent.[30] Similarly, real median household incomes between 2009 and 2015 rose by $1,528 among all groups and by $2,857 among whites, but they rose by only $945 among blacks.[31]

It would be unfair and misleading to discuss the country's economic performance under Obama outside of the context of the deep recession he inherited from his predecessor, George W. Bush. But Obama is not the first president to deal with a bad recession, and it is appropriate to compare his stewardship of an economic recovery with the performance

of other presidents. When economists Robert Barro and Tao
Jin looked at economic downturns in the United States and
forty-one other countries going back to the late nineteenth
century, they found that "the growth rate during a recovery relates positively to the magnitude of decline during the
downturn." On average during a recovery, they showed,
"an economy recoups about half the GDP lost during the
downturn." Moreover, arguing "that the recovery has been
weak because the downturn was severe or coincided with
a major financial crisis conflicts with the evidence, which
shows that a larger decline predicts a stronger recovery."[32]
Peter Ferrara of the National Bureau of Economic Research
noted in a 2016 paper that there have been twelve recessions
of various severity since the Great Depression and that the
average duration has been ten months. "When Obama came
into office, the recession, which started in December 2007,
was already 13 months old," wrote Ferrara. "That means the
recovery was already overdue. All he really had to do was
stay out of the way." Deep recessions in the United States
have generally been followed by strong recoveries. "Coming
out of a recession, the economy historically has grown faster
than normal for a while to catch up to its long-term economic
growth trendline," explained Ferrara. "By this metric, the
economy should have emerged in 2009 with a historic long-
term economic boom. To this day, however, seven years later,
that has yet to happen."[33]

One characteristic of recessions since the Great Depression

is that it has taken the economy around two years on average to recover job losses. After more severe downturns, however, jobs can take longer to come back. It took thirty-five months for the jobs that disappeared during the 1981-82 recession under President Ronald Reagan to be recovered. Obama, by comparison, oversaw by far the slowest recovery since World War II. The jobs lost in a recession that officially ended in the first year of his presidency would not be recovered for seventy-six months, or more than six years. "By early 2016, 98 months (more than eight years) after the recession started, under Obama's recovery the economy had created only 9.4 million more jobs on net," wrote Ferrara. "At that point in Reagan's recovery, the economy had created 21.5 million more jobs. Reagan's recovery, moreover, was 30 years ago, when the U.S. population, economy, and labor force were much smaller, making that job-creation figure comparatively even larger."[34]

The struggling economy's impact on blacks during Obama's presidency was not lost on civil rights groups. Although a large share of the jobs that did return were lower-wage jobs in which blacks tend to be overrepresented, six years after the recession officially ended the jobless rate for blacks was still above 9 percent and the jobless rate for black teens surpassed 31 percent.[35] The National Urban League's "State of Black America" report, which examines how blacks compare to whites "in areas of economics, health, education, social justice and civic engagement," found that blacks on balance were worse off in 2015 than in 2009.[36] "Things have improved from the dark days of the recession," said Marc Morial, the group's chief executive, shortly after Obama's presidency ended. "But the recovery for African Americans has not been as fast or as deep as it's been for whites."[37]

Such assessments notwithstanding, Obama remained hugely popular with black voters throughout his two-term presidency. His share of the black vote was 95 percent in 2008 and 93 percent four years later, and his job-approval rating among blacks hovered between the mid-nineties and low-eighties, or roughly forty points higher than what it averaged among all groups. But as a *Los Angeles Times* article on his legacy phrased it, "Polls have shown black people to be more satisfied with Obama the man and less with their progress under Obama the president."[38]

CHAPTER 3

False Black Power

―――――――――――――― ≳≲ ――――――――――――――

I F SUPPORT FOR Barack Obama among average black voters remained overwhelming throughout his time in office,
the chattering classes had a more complicated relationship
with the first black president. Liberal black intellectuals and
commentators defended Obama against political attacks
from the right, which were invariably ascribed to racial animus, but they also chided him for what they considered an
insufficient focus on the permanence of racial injustice in
America. Some black journalists seemed incapable of assess-
ing Obama's years in the White House through anything
other than a racial prism. The *Atlantic*'s Ta-Nehisi Coates
summarized the Obama presidency as "an eight-year campaign of consistent and open racism aimed at the leader of
the free world."[1]

One general complaint from the black left was that
Obama's public remarks were too hard on fellow blacks and
too easy on whites. This passage from his 2004 speech to the
Democratic National Convention, for example, rubbed many
black intellectuals the wrong way. "Go into any inner-city

neighborhood, and folks will tell you that government alone can't teach kids to learn," said Obama, who was a US senator at the time. "They know that parents have to teach, that children can't achieve unless we raise their expectations and turn off the television sets and eradicate the slander that says a black youth with a book is acting white."[2]

This type of talk was nothing new for Obama. As he said in an interview published several months after his convention speech, personal responsibility was a theme that he sounded on a regular basis, especially when addressing blacks:

> Every time I get an opportunity to speak to students, I deliver that message. I, for a number of years, have had to give commencement addresses at high school graduations, college graduations. When I'm speaking certainly before a minority audience, this is something that I always emphasize because I do not believe that money alone is going to solve our educational problems.
>
> We have to redouble our commitment to education within our own communities and within our homes, and raise the bar for our children in terms of what we expect from them. It's not enough that they just graduate. We should expect every young person out there to be getting A's. They can work harder. And we should turn off the television sets and curb the use of PlayStations.[3]

As president, some of Obama's most powerful comments on race focused on black self-help. "Keep setting an example for what it means to be a man," he told graduates of historically black Morehouse College in a 2013 commencement address. "Be the best husband to your wife, or your boyfriend, or your partner. Be the best father you can be to your children. Because nothing is more important." The president described the "heroic single mom" and "wonderful grandparents" who raised him but said he never got over not having his dad around. "I sure wish I had had a father who was not only present but involved," he said. "And so my whole life, I've tried to be for Michelle and my girls what my father was not for my mother and me. I want to break that cycle where a father is not at home—where a father is not helping to raise that son or daughter."[4]

During a town hall in 2014, Obama reflected on the self-defeating cultural attitudes that pervade black ghettos. "Sometimes African-Americans, in communities where I've worked, there's been the notion of 'acting white'—which sometimes is overstated, but there's an element of truth to it," he said before offering some examples. "If boys are reading too much, then, well, why are you doing that? Or why are you speaking so properly? And the notion that there's some authentic way of being black, that if you're going to be black you have to act a certain way and wear a certain kind of clothes—that has to go. Because there are a whole bunch of different ways for African-American men to be authentic."

Some liberal critics took umbrage at this notion that blacks are in any way responsible for their condition. "The 'acting white' libel is symptomatic of a more general perspective—a perspective that argues that an important factor explaining racial economic disparities is self-defeating or dysfunctional behavior on the part of blacks themselves," wrote William Darity, a professor of public policy at Duke University in a summary of the Obama presidency. "And Barack Obama continuously has trafficked in this perspective."[5]

A 2005 study published by Darity and two colleagues cast doubt on the well-documented links between black achievement and acting white, but their research methodology has been challenged. Just 125 students in eleven North Carolina schools were interviewed, and no direct questions about acting white were even asked. Moreover, Darity and his colleagues relied on what students reported about their own popularity, which is problematic because young people typically don't like to admit that they're unpopular. More rigorous studies that use much larger samples and don't rely on student self-reporting have shown empirically what Obama's anecdotes illustrated about the harsh treatment of bookish black students by their black peers. "The evidence supporting the 'acting white' thesis is fairly robust," wrote education scholar Stuart Buck. "We have over a dozen scholarly studies from the 1970s to 2008 confirming that the 'acting white' phenomenon does happen, while the studies that are supposed to disprove 'acting white' are fewer and less reliable."[6]

Other critics of Obama were less concerned about his comments on black anti-intellectualism per se and more bothered by the fact that they were voiced within earshot of so many whites. As John McWhorter of Columbia University noted, "Most blacks understand that 'the white man keeps me down' has become more a routine than an earnest statement," but there remains a "tacit rule" in the black community that "black responsibility and self-empowerment are not to be discussed at any length where whites can hear."[7]

In 2011, Philadelphia's black mayor, Michael Nutter, learned this firsthand. He gave a speech in a black church denouncing the flash mobs of black youths who for years had been rampaging through malls and parks and physically attacking innocent bystanders in the process. "You have damaged your own race," said Nutter. "Take those doggone hoodies down, especially in the summer. Pull your pants up and buy a belt because no one wants to see your underwear or the crack of your butt." Nutter's address focused on ghetto cultural deficiencies in general and black family structure in particular. "You know, you're not a father just because you have a kid or two or three. That doesn't make you a father," said the mayor. "A father is a person who's around to participate in a child's life. He's a teacher. Helps to guide and shape and mold that young person, someone for that young person to talk to, to share with—their ups and their downs, their fears, and their concerns. A father has to provide instruction to a young boy on how to become a good man." If you're only providing monetary support, "you're just an ATM," said Nutter, and "that's not being a father."

Nutter said that fatherless homes are "a particular problem in the black communities" and ultimately a burden on society. "We have too many men making too many babies that they don't want to take care of, and then we end up dealing with your children. We're not running a big baby-sitting service. We're running a big government and a great city. Take care of your children—all of 'em." The mayor said that negative perceptions of blacks won't change if black antisocial behavior doesn't change, and he concluded his remarks with a pointed message to young blacks:

> If you want all of us—black, white, or any other color—if you want us to respect you, if you want us to look at you in a different way, if you want us not to be afraid to walk down the same side of the street with you, if you want folks not to jump out of the elevator when you get on, if you want folks to stop following you around in stores when you're out shopping, if you want somebody to offer you a job or an internship somewhere, if you don't want folks to be looking in or trying to go in a different direction when they see two or twenty of you coming down the street, then stop acting like idiots and fools, out in the streets of the city of Philadelphia. Just cut it out.[8]

Members of the black church where Nutter spoke stood and chanted, "Buy a belt, buy a belt!" in appreciation of this plain, honest truth telling. The black smart set, by contrast, was not only unpersuaded but enraged. A local columnist accused him of saying what his "white constituents" wanted to hear.[9] A Columbia University professor insisted that poverty is the root cause of black social degeneration and that Nutter should have focused on "structural barriers" and "the need for political struggle to correct those barriers."[10] It's a typical illustration of the wide disconnect between the preferences of black elites and the attitudes of everyday blacks, who feel less need to tiptoe around racial realities.

Obama was not oblivious to this criticism, which might explain why he sometimes dialed down the self-help message and even became defensive. "There have been times where some thoughtful and sometimes not so thoughtful African-American commentators have gotten on both Michelle and me, suggesting that we are not addressing enough sort of institutional barriers and racism, and we're engaging in sort of up-by-the-bootstraps, Booker T. Washington messages that let the larger society off the hook," he told *New Yorker* magazine in 2014. "I always tell people to go read some of Dr. King's writings about the African-American community. For that matter, read Malcolm X. . . . There's no contradiction to say that there are issues of personal responsibility that have to be addressed, while still acknowledging that some of the specific pathologies in the African-American community are a direct result of our history."[11]

Another common criticism of Obama, which he referenced in the above quote, is that he didn't do enough to highlight and combat the white racism that liberals believe to be by far the biggest barrier to black prosperity. "I was once a vocal surrogate for Obama," wrote Michael Eric Dyson, a sociology professor and television commentator. "But I grew disillusioned with his timid response to racial crisis, with how willing he was to disclaim his racial affiliation, and more grievously, his shirking of his political duty—'I'm not the president of black America,' he has said."[12]

Fellow academic Cornel West told CNN, "I would say the first black president has become the first niggerized black president." Asked to explain the ugly neologism, he offered that "a niggerized black person is a black person who is afraid and scared and intimidated when it comes to putting a spotlight on white supremacy and fighting against white supremacy." For West, Obama's foremost duty as a black president was to tackle racial bias, and his inability or unwillingness to do that (to the satisfaction of people like Cornel West) made him not only a failure but a kind of race traitor. "You can't talk about wealth and inequality, you can't talk about education, you can't talk about massive unemployment and under employment and you can't talk about drones being dropped on people in other parts of the world without talking about white supremacy and its ways in which it operates," said the professor.[13]

After Donald Trump's election, the *New Republic* published a discussion of Obama's legacy that included two black historians, Nell Painter of Princeton and Annette Gordon-Reed of Harvard. Asked how much responsibility Obama bears for Trump's victory, Painter responded: "I don't think it has anything to do with him personally, except that he's a black man. The election of Trump was a gut-level response to what many Americans interpreted as an insult eight years ago, and have been seething against ever since. The only way you can see Trump as somehow Obama's fault is Obama's very being. It's ontological." Gordon-Reed agreed, adding that "for the first black president, there were all kinds of psychic things going on that just don't apply for a 'regular' person."[14] For black progressives, Obama's race didn't prevent him from being elected, yet his race somehow was the main factor in his inability to advance his agenda to their liking.

It's possible that these various reactions reflect the mixed messages sent by Obama before and during his presidency. In his keynote address at the 2004 Democratic National Convention, the speech that first brought him national attention, he waxed inclusive. "There is not a liberal America and a conservative America; there is a United States of America," he said. "There is not a black America and white America and Latino America; there is a United States of America." As president, Obama at times pushed back at claims that opposition to his policies was racially motivated, as his defenders often insisted. Early in his first term, during an appearance on David Letterman's television talk show, the president was asked if his critics were simply antiblack, as former President Jimmy Carter and Democrats in Congress had been suggesting. "I think it's important to realize that I was actually black before the election," Obama quipped, and then told Letterman that he thought the criticism mostly reflected policy differences and came with the job. "One of the things that you sign up for in politics is that folks yell at you."

During an interview with the *Atlantic* just before leaving office, Obama was asked if the Republicans in Congress who consistently opposed his agenda were motivated by racism. He replied that he felt the GOP was driven by partisan politics. "If Republicans didn't cooperate" he said, "and there was not a portrait of bipartisan cooperation and a functional federal government, then the party in power would pay the price and they could win back the Senate and/or the House. That wasn't an inaccurate political calculation." Asked if racism played into that calculation, Obama demurred. "I do remember watching Bill Clinton get impeached and Hillary Clinton being accused of killing Vince Foster," he responded. "And if you ask them, I'm sure they would say, 'No, actually what you're experiencing is not because you're black, it's because you're a Democrat.'"[15]

At the same time, however, Obama's top surrogates regularly accused the president's critics of racial bias. Vice President Joe Biden told a mostly black audience in 2012 that Republicans want to put you "back in chains."[16] Attorney General Eric Holder gave speeches in which he accused voter identification proponents of trying to disenfranchise blacks, even though polling has shown that a majority of all groups, including blacks, support voter identification laws.[17] Holder also told ABC News that "there's a certain level of vehemence, it seems to me, that's directed at me [and] directed at the president." He added: "You know, people talking about taking their country back. . . . There's a certain racial component to this for some people. I don't think this is the thing that is a main driver, but for some there's a racial animus." If the president was bothered by these statements, he didn't make a habit of saying so publicly.

Nor was Obama himself above racial pandering, as when he commented after the 2012 shooting death of Trayvon Martin, a black teenager in Florida, that "if I had a son, he'd look like Trayvon." In 2009, he suggested that the arrest of Henry Louis Gates, a black Harvard professor who was briefly taken into custody following an altercation with police, may have been racially motivated. "I don't know, not having been there and not seeing all the facts, what role race played in that," said Obama after being asked about the Gates incident. "What I think we know separate and apart from this incident is that there is a long history in this country of African-Americans and Latinos being stopped by law enforcement disproportionately. That's just a fact."[18]

Obama's previous calls for colorblindness also did not stop him or Holder from making common cause with controversial individuals like Al Sharpton, one of the most racially polarizing public figures in America over the past three decades. Sharpton traffics in racial discord, not harmony, yet the president and attorney general spoke at annual conventions for Sharpton's organization, the National Action Network, and the activist was a regular visitor to the Obama White House.

The Obama era featured several highly publicized police shootings of black men, which the president exploited to push pet reforms for a criminal justice system that he considered stacked against blacks. After police officer Darren Wilson was acquitted by a multiracial jury in the 2014 shooting death of Michael Brown in Ferguson, Missouri, the president said the decision should be respected but that "there are Americans who are deeply disappointed, even angry. It's an understandable reaction." Why "understandable" in his view? Well, as Obama told an NAACP conference in 2015, "The bottom line is that in too many places, black boys and black men, Latino boys and Latino men experience being treated differently under the law." As evidence, he noted that blacks and Hispanics make up just 30 percent of the population but 60 percent of inmates.

Omitting black crime rates from discussions about black incarceration rates, as Obama and his supporters often did, is misleading but common—especially in the media. See, for example, the lengthy July 2016 *Washington Post* story offering a detailed breakdown of police shootings by race but no similarly detailed racial breakdown of criminal behavior.[19] Law professor Michelle Alexander's 2010 bestseller, *The New Jim Crow*, is more of the same at book length. What often go unmentioned are the numerous empirical studies demonstrating that black arrests and incarceration rates reflect black behavior, not systemic bias. "Contrary to frequently voiced accusations and despite voluminous literature intent upon demonstrating discrimination at every turn, there is almost no reliable evidence of racial bias in the criminal justice system's handling of ordinary violent and non-violent offenses," wrote University of Pennsylvania Law Professor Amy Wax. "Rather, the facts overwhelmingly show that blacks go to prison more often because blacks commit more crimes."[20]

A 2016 paper released by Harvard economist Roland Fryer, who later said he had expected to find racial bias in police shootings,[21] instead discovered that "blacks are 23.8 percent less likely to be shot at by police relative to whites" and that "Hispanics are 8.5 percent less likely," based on an analysis of data from one of several cities he studied.[22] Fryer did find racial disparities in nonlethal uses of force by police but cautioned against automatically ascribing those differences to racial bias, noting that "the data does more to provide a more compelling case that there is no discrimination in officer-involved shootings than it does to illuminate the reasons behind racial differences in non-lethal uses of force."[23] And no wonder. One analysis of New York City's controversial "stop and frisk" program, which coincided with a record drop in violent crime but was criticized by opponents as racist, found that "black pedestrians were stopped at a rate that is 20 to 30 percent lower than their representation in crime-suspect descriptions"—descriptions by civilians, not police.[24] Fryer's study, which examined more than 1,300 shootings since 2000 in Florida, Texas, and California, found that officers in Dallas, Austin, Houston, Los Angeles, and several Florida counties were "47.4% less likely to discharge their firearms before being attacked if the suspect is black" than if the suspect is white.[25] Moreover, black and white victims of police shootings were equally likely to have been armed, according to Fryer's findings, which further undercut the popular liberal narrative that police are gunning for blacks out of racial prejudice.

Confronted with these high-profile incidents between law enforcement and black suspects, Obama also could have pointed out that police shootings have been on the decline for decades and are statistically rare. There is no comprehensive federal database on police shootings, and perhaps one should be devised. Currently, some police departments collect and report more extensive information than others. But, the data we do have, shows that police are involved in a tiny percentage of black shooting deaths each year. One economist has calculated "that police are six times as likely to be killed by black civilians than black civilians are to be killed by police."[26] In the first six months of 2016, there were around 2,100 shootings in Chicago, but police carried out just nine of them. By the end of the year, there had been more than 4,300 shootings in the Second City. Almost all the victims were black, with civilians carrying out more than 99 percent of the shootings.[27]

In New York, which is home to the nation's largest police force, detailed records of police shootings date to 1971. That year, cops shot 314 people, 93 of them fatally. By 1991, police shootings had fallen to 108 with 27 fatalities. And in 2015, New York cops shot 23 people, killing 8. That's a 92 percent reduction in police shootings and a 91 percent reduction in fatalities over a forty-four-year span in America's largest city. "As long as armed criminals walk the streets, the number of police shootings will never be reduced to zero. And as long as cops are human, there will be mistakes, misjudgments and even criminal activity on the part of some police officers," wrote Charles Campisi, a former head of internal affairs for the New York City Police Department. "Any time a cop shoots someone without justification, he or she must be held to strict account. But the bottom line on this difficult issue is clear: Despite the public perception, American law-enforcement officers generally do a good job of not shooting people. Though we must never stop trying to do better, dealing effectively with the problem requires having a clear picture of its actual extent."[28]

≳≲

Obama showed little interest in providing any clarity or context on racial disparities and instead chose to focus on doing what was politically expedient. Police are public servants, and police abuse is a serious matter that should never be downplayed or ignored. But the idea that police behavior in ghetto communities is the foremost problem—which is what activist groups like Black Lives Matter have alleged and politicians like Barack Obama have lent credence to—is rooted in liberal identity politics, not reality. The administration investigated nearly two dozen police forces around the country over allegations of civil rights abuses.[29] And the president regularly invoked racial and ethnic bias when discussing drug laws, sentencing guidelines, and mass incarceration while rarely if ever mentioning the significant racial differences in criminal activity.

Criticism from black progressives notwithstanding, Obama played the race card plenty. He accused conservatives on the Supreme Court of weakening black voting rights and advocated for racial double standards in college admissions. He reflexively sided against law enforcement in local incidents involving black suspects and sympathized with antipolice Black Lives Matter activists—even appointing one of their leaders to a federal task force on policing. His support for looser drug laws and his decision to commute record numbers of prison sentences undermined law enforcement and gave the impression that he cared more about lawbreakers than their victims. Under Obama, federal housing officials forced

upscale suburbs to import low-income minorities or risk losing government funding, even when there was no evidence
that these communities were discriminating against anyone
who could afford to move in,[30] and education officials pres-
sured schools to discipline students based on race, not behavior.[31] In the final months of his presidency, Obama made
overt and repeated racial appeals to black voters to support
Hillary Clinton as his successor, even declaring that he would
consider it a "personal insult" if they didn't rally behind her.[32]

Given Clinton's underperformance in the election among
blacks in critical states that Trump won—Michigan, Pennsylvania, Ohio—Obama must have left office insulted. And
his administration's racial politics almost certainly harmed
racial discourse. By 2016, race relations had reached their
lowest point in nearly a quarter century. In a *Washington
Post*–ABC News poll taken halfway through the final year of
the Obama presidency, 63 percent of respondents said race
relations were "generally bad," and a majority agreed they
were "getting worse."[33] A *New York Times* poll from around
the same time showed similar results. "Sixty-nine percent of
Americans say race relations are generally bad, one of the
highest levels of discord since the 1992 riots in Los Angeles
during the Rodney King case," the paper reported. "Racial
discontent is at its highest point in the Obama presidency
and at the same level as after the riots touched off by the
1992 acquittal of Los Angeles police officers charged in Mr.
King's beating.[34]

≳≲

Obama's presidency suggests that attempts to advance blacks through heightened group identity and us-against-them posturing can be just as ineffective as the black political power route has been. And there is reason to believe that these left-wing prescriptions for lifting blacks could become even less effective with time. Today, America is much more racially and ethnically diverse than it was a half-century ago, and demographers say the trend is accelerating. In 2010, twenty-two of the nation's one hundred largest metropolitan areas were minority white. That was up from fourteen in 2000 and just five in 1990. In twenty years, there could be no racial majority any longer in America.[35] In an increasingly pluralistic country, does it make sense to push a politics based on group consciousness and racial spoils?

Just after Obama's 2008 election, race scholar Shelby Steele posed a series of rhetorical questions that were on the minds of many Americans. "Does his victory mean that America is now officially beyond racism?" wrote Steele. "Can the good Revs. [Jesse] Jackson and [Al] Sharpton now safely retire to the seashore? Will the Obama victory dispel the twin stigmas that have tormented black and white Americans for so long—that blacks are inherently inferior and whites inherently racist? Doesn't a black in the Oval Office put the lie to both black inferiority and white racism? Doesn't it imply a 'post-racial' America?"

Steele himself was skeptical. "There is nothing to suggest that Obama will lead America into true post-racialism," he predicted. "His campaign style revealed a tweaker of the status quo, not a revolutionary. Culturally and racially, he is likely to leave America pretty much where he found her." Regarding what an Obama presidency would mean for blacks, Steele was even more pessimistic:

> Won't an Obama presidency at last lead us [blacks] across a centuries-old gulf of alienation into the recognition that America really is our country? Might this milestone not infuse black America with a new American nationalism? And wouldn't this be revolutionary in itself? Like most Americans, I would love to see an Obama presidency nudge things in this direction. But the larger reality is the profound disparity between black and white Americans that will persist even under the glow of an Obama presidency. The black illegitimacy rate remains at 70%. Blacks did worse on the SAT in 2000 than in 1990. Fifty-five percent of all federal prisoners are black, though we are only 13% of the population. The academic achievement gap between blacks and whites persists even for the black middle class. All this disparity will continue to accuse blacks of inferiority and whites of racism—thus refueling our racial politics—despite the level of melanin in the president's skin.[36]

Turns out, as Steele predicted, that it wasn't Obama's election itself that moved us toward some kind of postracialism but rather how the nation's first black president chose to govern. Opposition to America's racist and sexist past has defined liberalism since the 1960s and led to "today's markers of white guilt—political correctness, identity politics, environmental orthodoxy, the diversity cult and so on," wrote Steele shortly after Obama left office. "Perhaps the Obama presidency was the culmination of the age of white guilt, so that this guiltiness has entered its denouement." This liberalism, Steele added,

> evolved within a society shamed by its past. But that shame has weakened now. Our new conservative president rolls his eyes when he is called a racist, and we all—liberal and conservative alike—know that he isn't one. The jig is up. Bigotry exists, but it is far down on the list of problems that minorities now face. I grew up black in segregated America, where it was hard to find an open door. It's harder now for young blacks to find a closed one.[37]

A few days after Trump's surprise victory over Hillary Clinton, I walked around New York City's Harlem neighborhood and got reactions from a couple dozen black residents. Postelection street demonstrations were occurring in major cities across the country almost daily. The media tended to present the protests as spontaneous displays of outrage from average citizens over the election results, and some of them surely were. But it's also true that many of the rallies were being organized and supported by professional agitators at outfits like MoveOn.org and Al Sharpton's National Action Network.[38] Minorities were said to be especially concerned about a Trump presidency due to his harsh campaign rhetoric directed at Latino immigrants and blacks.

However, the people I spoke with in Harlem weren't shocked by the outcome or overly concerned about their future under a Trump administration. I didn't find any Trump supporters, but neither did I find anyone interested in taking to the streets to oppose his election. For the most part, people told me that they would give Trump a chance to do the things he said he would do—such as reduce crime and protect entitlement programs. And unlike so many black public intellectuals and activists, they expressed a healthy skepticism of politicians and government solutions. "He said he'd protect Medicare. I can go along with that," said a retiree who was having a smoke with a friend outside of a barbershop. "He said he'd get rid of the Bloods and the Crips and the gangs— get them out of here. I like that. If he does those two things, he's my man. If he don't deliver on that, he's just another politician." A minister sitting in front of his storefront church also weighed in on the prevalence of inner-city street violence but concluded that "we know the president can't do much about crime. It has to start at home with the families, the

parents, the fathers." A woman getting her hair done in a
beauty salon was even more forthright. "I don't think Trump
is really thinking about black people's problems," she told me
as some of the other customers listening in nodded. "Even
if he was, he can't solve them. Obama scouldn't solve them
even though he really wanted to, so Trump certainly can't.
But let's see what he does."

This sobriety of November 2016 contrasted sharply with
the headiness of November 2008, when so many people
viewed the incoming president as a kind of political savior—a
view Obama didn't exactly discourage. For blacks, however,
Obama's presidency turned out to be more of a distraction
from the reality that political power can't compensate for
what is missing culturally. History, including black history,
has offered little reason to expect faster and more sustained
black progress from the prioritization of political solutions
over the development of human capital. Successful groups
in America—as measured by income, academic accomplishment, and professional attainment—have developed certain
attitudes, habits, and behaviors. Some groups developed these
traits before they came to America; others learned them after
they arrived. But the cultural development tended to precede
the eventual prosperity. Today's black leaders are preoccu-
pied with developing excuses, and those excuses often center
on white villainy in one form or another.

"Many tell us that white opposition to blacks is so
uniquely fierce that it is useless to compare us to others,"

wrote John McWhorter. "But how useless is it to compare us to ourselves?" As far back as the late 1800s, "American cities typically had thriving black business districts reproducing white America down to the last detail, including excellent schools—Bronzeville, Chicago; the Auburn Avenue district in Atlanta; the Shaw district in Washington, DC; even Harlem before the 1940s." As McWhorter explained:

> These people were no strangers to racism, which was overt and hostile across America. They could not shop in many white stores or stay in most white hotels; they were barred from most prestigious positions in the mainstream world; they read regularly of lynchings; and interracial relationships and marriages were all but unheard of and condemned anyone who dared them to acrid social ostracization. And yet the very people who lived in that world would be baffled at the consensus among their descendants that whites' biases rend us powerless to shape our destinies for the better.[39]

They would be baffled and then some. The 1913 edition of the *Negro Almanac*, which marked the fiftieth anniversary of the Emancipation Proclamation, boasted that "no other emancipated people have made so great a progress in short a time." It elaborated by comparing the progress of freed slaves in the United States to that of Russian serfs who had been emancipated around the same time, in 1861. Fifty years after being freed, fourteen million former serfs had accumulated some $500 million, or $36 per capita, and 30 percent could read and write. By comparison, after fifty years of freedom "the 10 million Negroes in the United States have accumulated over $700,000,000 worth of property, or about $70 per capita," the almanac reported, using Census data, and "70 percent of them have some education in books."⁴⁰ Robert Higgs, an economic historian, wrote in 2008 that even if black literacy a half-century after emancipation reached only 50 percent, "the magnitude of the accomplishment is still striking, especially when one recalls the overwhelming obstacles blocking black educational efforts. For a large population to transform itself from virtually unlettered to more than half literate in 50 years ranks as an accomplishment seldom witnessed in human history."⁴¹

In 1865, black entrepreneurs were engaged in just twelve different types of commercial enterprises, which included hairdressing, sailmaking, shopkeeping, shoe repair, and catering. By 1917, blacks would own and operate some two hundred different kinds of businesses as they quit the rural South and headed for nearby cities or urban centers in the North and West. In the 1910s, the black populations of Los Angeles, Chicago, Miami, Cleveland, and Detroit grew by between 105 percent (Los Angeles) and 611 percent (Detroit). The migration continued in the 1920s, when small- and mid-sized cities like Youngstown, Ohio; Durham, North Carolina; and

Buffalo, New York, also saw their black populations double and triple in size. The black population of Gary, Indiana, climbed from 383 in 1910 to 17,922 in 1930.[42]

According to a business directory, there were already around two hundred black businesses operating in twenty-seven different fields in Chicago alone by 1885. A history of the city's black Bronzeville neighborhood noted that the "rapid growth of the Negro community between 1915 and 1929 was accompanied by expansion in all types of Negro-owned businesses," from beauty salons and groceries to banks and insurance companies. "In 1938, Negroes in Bronzeville owned and operated some 2,600 business enterprises," most of which were small retail and service outfits catering to people in less desirable communities.[43]

Low wages, poor working conditions, and even near-total exclusion from certain jobs—such as clerical positions—couldn't stop a black middle class from emerging in Milwaukee, Wisconsin, between 1915 and 1932. "The number of blacks engaged in professional, business, and clerical occupations increased from 80 in 1910 to 301 by 1930," wrote historian Joe William Trotter. "This included an increase of 120.7 percent between 1920 and 1930. Black proprietors led the list with 3.5 percent of the total labor force in 1930. Professional people (3.4 percent) and clerical workers (1.2 percent)." Williams noted that while the number may seem insignificant, the trend was not. "With their small percentages in business and professional pursuits from the beginning of the period, the number of Afro-American proprietors and professionals expanded at a rate faster than that of the city at large."[44]

The progress of blacks after leaving slavery and prior to the civil rights legislation of the 1960s doesn't receive a lot of attention because it undermines a prevailing and politically useful narrative on the left. That narrative, which is seldom challenged, insists that black underachievement is primarily a function of white racism, that blacks need special favors like affirmative action to improve their lot, and that black integration of political institutions is essential to black advancement. These arguments serve the interest of the people making them, whether those people are racial and ethnic leaders trying to remain influential or political leaders trying to win votes. Still, black history itself offers a compelling counternarrative that ideally would inform our post-Obama racial inequality debates.

In his 1907 book, *The Negro in Business*, Booker T. Washington reported that between 1860 and 1900, black homeownership rates grew from infinitesimal to nearly 22 percent. Additionally, 74.2 percent of black homeowners completely owned their residences as of 1900, versus only 68 percent of white families. "I am unaware that history records such an example of substantial growth in civilization in a time so short," wrote Washington. "Here is the unique fact that from a penniless population, just out of slavery, that placed a premium on thriftlessness, 372,414 owners of homes have emerged, and of these 255,156 are known to own their homes absolutely free of encumbrance."[45]

Between 1950 and 1960 in New York City, which had the largest black urban population in the country and where racial discrimination in employment was lawful and commonplace, the number of black accountants rose by more than 200 percent. The number of engineers increased by 134 percent. The number of schoolteachers grew by 125 percent. The rise in black physicians (56 percent), lawyers (55 percent), nurses (90 percent), and social workers (146 percent) were also striking.[46] The Civil Rights Act and Voting Rights Act would not be passed until the mid-1960s, and there is no intention here to minimize the importance of that legislation in making America a more fair and just country. Nor is there any intention to diminish the efforts of so many good people who fought and sometimes died in that effort. But the fact that blacks were entering white-collar professions so rapidly before those landmark bills were passed tells us what they were able to accomplish even during Jim Crow. "The growth of racial segregation in the 1950s did not keep Black residential options [in New York] from expanding," wrote civil rights historian Martha Biondi. "From 1940 to 1950 the earnings of Black workers tripled, with a substantial number meeting the income eligibility of homeownership" suggested by the government. In 1953, a real estate journal called blacks "than nation's newest middle class."[47] The same year, *Time* wrote, "The signs of Negro prosperity are everywhere. On the rooftops of Manhattan's Harlem grows that bare ugly forest of TV antennae which has become a new symbol of middle-class achievement."[48]

Black progress during this period was not limited to New York City. The scholars Stephan and Abigail Thernstrom reported that nationwide the number of black teachers quadrupled between 1940 and 1970, and the number of "social workers and registered nurses rose even more, from under 10,000 to almost 110,000, with much of the expansion preceding the Great Society programs of the late 1960s." The Thernstroms added that whether this progress would have continued without the racial preference policies that later took effect in the 1970s "is open to debate. But it certainly cannot be assumed that the progress that has been made since then could not possibly have occurred without affirmative action."[49]

The great migrations out of the rural South that began during World War I changed the demographic profile of blacks as well as the country. At least 90 percent of blacks still lived in the South in 1900, and three-quarters of working blacks were employed in agriculture or domestic services as late as 1910. The move to cities in the North, West, Midwest, and even the South often meant better schools and higher-paying jobs. More than fifty thousand blacks moved to Chicago between

1916 and 1917. "Coming from the South, where they are accustomed to work for a few cents a day or a few dollars a week, to an industrial center where they can earn that much in an hour or a day, they have the feeling that this city is really the land overflowing with milk and honey," said one contemporary observer. "In the occupations in which they are now employed, many of them are engaged in skilled labor, receiving the same and, in some cases, greater compensation than was paid white men in such a position prior to the outbreak of the war." Historian Robert Weems noted that blacks who stayed in Dixie but moved to urban areas also saw their wages rise during this period. "Thus, in the South, as in the North, prized black workers were able to command higher salaries," he wrote. "Even in the traditionally oppressive (for blacks) Mississippi, the wages of African Americans living in urban areas increased by from 10 to 100 percent."[50]

A second and larger exodus of blacks from the South coincided with the start of World War II. More than a million blacks left the region in the 1940s, and another million left in the 1950s. These were decades of strong economic growth and job creation in the United States, and blacks were progressing in absolute terms and relative to whites notwithstanding all manner of de facto and de jure discrimination. Between 1939 and 1960, median incomes for black men rose from $460 to $3,075, or by 568.5 percent. For white men, they grew from $1,112 to $5,137, or by 362 percent over the same period. The story was similar for black women, who saw their median incomes rise steadily in the 1940s and 1950s, from $246 in 1939 to $1,276 in 1960. That represented a 418.7 percent increase over a two-decade period when white women saw their median incomes go up by only 275.3 percent.[51]

≥≤

Education also played a critical role in this advancement. Blacks were narrowing the income gap because they were also narrowing the learning gap. Discrimination kept blacks out of certain fields and occupations, to be sure, but so did a lack of schooling necessary to join certain professions. Even without discrimination, blacks would have had difficulty competing for white-collar jobs. Blacks began to address this situation in earnest in the first half of the twentieth century and decades before the existence of affirmative action policies that would later receive undeserved credit for creating a black middle class. In fact, the "rise of blacks into professional and other high-level occupation was greater in the years preceding passage of the Civil Rights Act of 1964 than in the years following the passage of that act," explained Thomas Sowell. "Similarly, and despite a widespread tendency to see the rise of blacks out of poverty as due to the civil rights movement and government social programs of the 1960s, in reality the rise of blacks out of poverty was greater in the two decades preceding 1960 than the decades that followed." Between

1940 and 1960, blacks and whites alike increased their years of schooling, but the racial gap narrowed from four years to less than two years. Elaborating on the economic significance of this development, Sowell wrote:

> As of 1940, more than four-fifths of black families—87 percent, in fact—lived below the official poverty level. By 1960, this had fallen to 47 percent. In other words, the poverty rate among blacks had been nearly cut in half before either the civil rights revolution or the Great Society social programs began in the 1960s. The continuation of this trend can hardly be automatically credited to these political developments, though such claims are often made, usually ignoring the pre-existing trends whose momentum could hardly have been expected to stop in the absence of such legislation. By 1970, the poverty rate among blacks had fallen to 30 percent—a welcome development, but by no means unprecedented. A decade after that, with the rise of affirmative action in the intervening years, the poverty rate among black families had fallen to 29 percent. Even if one attributes all of this one percent decline to government policy, it does not compare to the dramatic declines in poverty among blacks when the only major change was the rise in their education.[52]

The tragedy today is that this black history—this story of black triumph over adversity in the face of near-impossible odds—is downplayed by most black leaders, to the extent that it's even acknowledged. Black elected officials and activists can be expected to say and do what is in their own interests, even if pursuing those interests leaves blacks as a group worse off. Hence, the Congressional Black Caucus pushes for political solutions regardless of whether a problem really calls for more government help. Its members are rewarded with votes for winning special favors for blacks and for blaming black problems on others, so that is their focus. Al Sharpton and the NAACP leadership show little interest in data that demonstrates tremendous black socioeconomic advancement during segregation because they have spent decades insisting that blacks can't advance until racism in all its forms has been eradicated. If racial prejudice is no longer a significant barrier to black upward mobility and doesn't explain today's racial disparities, the civil rights old guard is irrelevant.

Today, black people hear plenty about what they can't achieve due to racism and very little about what they have achieved in the past notwithstanding brutal and sometimes lethal bigotry. Yes, racism—in one form or another and to various degrees—has been a constant for blacks since the first slaves were brought to America, but the amount and quality of human capital among blacks has not been constant. After emancipation, blacks set about acquiring the values, habits, and skills necessary to thrive in a capitalist system. The going was tough and the progress was slow at times, but the gains were steady and undeniable. Racial gaps in education, incomes, and professional attainment were closing—doing so during a period when many whites were openly biased and the welfare of blacks wasn't exactly a government priority. The conventional attitudes of blacks toward marriage, parenting, school, and work a century ago aided and abetted this unprecedented black economic advancement and complicate liberal claims that black antisocial behavior in the twenty-first century is a "legacy" of slavery and Jim Crow. Since the 1960s, the focus on developing human capital has shifted to a focus on acquiring political power—a false sense of power—and this change in priorities has coincided with dramatic changes in black trends over the past half-century. In some areas, social and economic progress has merely slowed, but in other cases it has stalled completely or even been reversed. The Obama era was more evidence of the limits of this strategy. If blacks want to begin replenishing that human capital—true power—they shouldn't look to politicians. They should look to their own past.

PART 2

≥≤

Dissenting Points of View

CHAPTER 4

Keeping Up With the Leftists
New Observations for Variations on the Theme

≳≲

JOHN MCWHORTER

J ASON RILEY'S CRITIQUE is fundamentally correct. Especially invaluable is his point that black Americans achieved so very much when racism was more open, immediate, and implacable than they have since the civil rights revolutions of the 1960s. Riley's more specific point is equally unavoidable: the fundamental idea that black people must have a certain amount of political "representation" as a precondition for significant achievement is a fallacy. Many groups have achieved before they had such "representation," including black people before the 1960s.

≳≲

MY QUIBBLES WITH RILEY'S argumentation arise largely from the fact that his approach sometimes proceeds more as if it were about twenty years ago than today. The race debate remains the circular, performative sham that it was then, and if anything, it has moved even further in that direction of late. However, the cast in the production has changed somewhat. For example, I doubt that in 2017 there is much use in holding two figures like Jesse Jackson and Al Sharpton as key exhibits as to what ails black America. Both men are faded presences, and, crucially, they have produced no heirs.

Jackson quietly lost real influence once it was revealed in 2001 that he had fathered a child out of wedlock during the very time he was "ministering" to Bill Clinton during the scandal over the latter man's love life. I can barely recall the last race episode in American life in which Jackson played any significant role. Sharpton is now hosting a low-rated television show largely kept on the air as a kind of window dressing for its leftist-inclined network, and to the extent that he represents black people abused or killed by the police, he does this in much more pacific fashion than in the old days and has done so for long enough now that it's somewhat unfair to maintain judging him as if he were the race-baiting firebrand in a sweatsuit that he was during the Reagan administration.

In any case, can we really say that any sonorous ministers are leading black thought today? Or, on Riley's charge that President Obama's statements about race and policing made our race debate more bitter, could a few sentences uttered by even the president really have had such a decisive impact? The idea that Obama stirred up the pot on race in America is, I suspect, a mistake caused by a coincidence: Twitter and

Facebook broke out in 2009, right when Obama took the reins. Social media have transformed the race debate decisively; Obama was just along for the ride.

On the contrary, the targets of Riley's animus in this vein should be a certain cadre of public intellectuals who have a more vivid presence in black lives than Jackson or Sharpton ever did beyond their pulpits in their cities of residence. Thinkers such as Ta-Nehisi Coates, Michael Eric Dyson, Melissa Harris-Perry, and others express their views on television regularly, accessible around the clock on iPhones and shared on social media. It is these people, read widely (and in the case of Coates's *Between the World and Me*, assigned to college students nationwide) who play a key role, along with white supporters such as the hosts of shows on National Public Radio and MSNBC, in shaping what is perceived to be the "proper" view on race. Notably, these people do reproduce themselves—beyond the ones at the level of the three I just mentioned are a crop of others just a level below and legions of smart young writers eager to become them. Note that the equivalents of these figures in the 1980s and 1990s never had the household-name influence of today's hot black public thinkers—if they started out in the public sphere today, people like bell hooks and Lani Guinier would be rock stars of similar caliber; they just came along before today's technology.

≥≤

Meanwhile, Riley is quite correct that "the major barrier to black progress today is not racial discrimination and hasn't been for decades. The challenge for blacks is to better position themselves to take advantage of existing opportunities, and that involves addressing the antisocial, self-defeating behaviors and habits and attitudes endemic to the black underclass." However, his argument would have a better chance of convincing the fence-sitters (and maybe even some leftward) if he addressed the full counterargument typical from his opponents.

That is, the claim is no longer that black America owes its condition just to slavery and Jim Crow. Even the true believers always likely knew that this argument was more of a stretch every year that passed after 1964. These days—especially since the publication of William Julius Wilson's key books in the late 1980s and early 1990s—the idea is that slavery and Jim Crow were followed by factory relocation, depriving poor blacks of stable low-skill work, and redlining, which is thought to have consigned black neighborhoods to social oblivion by concentrating too many black people in the same place (that smart people call it supporting black people to accept this barbarously condescending argument is Exhibit A that academic black thought is a religion in the guise of a paradigm).

One may perceive the hollowness of the redlining argument and the one about factory relocation (i.e., so many poor people, including black ones both native and immigrant, got other kinds of jobs), but to leave them unaddressed is to make what is technically an incomplete case to the other side. Not long ago, if one criticized rap, there was ever someone on the edge of their seat waiting to object that "it's not all like that" and rattle off a list of their favorite "conscious" rappers who avoided the "gangsta" routines. In the same way, today if a conservative says that black America can't use slavery and Jim Crow as an excuse anymore, it's considered the height of wisdom to object that factory relocation and redlining had equally pernicious effects. The latter argument, for example, was most of what was seen as so valuable in Coates's *Atlantic* article on reparations, which otherwise rehashed an argument that had been worn out and put to rest just fifteen years before.

Thus, the mistake today is not people "conflating the past with the present" and pretending that nothing has changed since 1960. The idea, rather, is that modern conditions are uniquely unsurmountable—that the descendants of African slaves today face conditions that make them the first humans unable to avoid social catastrophe short of a profound and complete overturning of their society's sociological mechanics. That, when stated explicitly, is a clearly weak argument. However, it must be aired and presented to the opponents for comment: otherwise, we argue past them, or worse, allow it to appear, from their passionate objections loaded with portentous terminology and buzz words, that they have defeated us.

≳≲

I fear, also, that the roots of the left's fantastical approach to race issues are deeper, and thus harder to change, than a mere matter of seeking political power. I'm not sure if there are actually career politicians who consciously stir up anti-racist grievance in order to maintain their constituency, but if there are, this group is but a sliver of the body of people who pretend that what black people require to succeed is a racism-free America with a perfectly level playing field (and, as I have said, we overestimate the extent to which such celebrities affect general black thought). Whites maintain this odd blend of utopianism and fatalism as a way of proving their morality; blacks maintain it as a substitute for a true sense of racial pride. Neither the white college kid protesting along with black students, the black middle manager who thrills to the teachings of Coates and Dyson, nor most listeners of National Public Radio are "poverty pimps" motivated by political power. Rather, what drives them is a sense that portraying black people as defined by victimhood is a way of being a good person.

≳≲

My comments here are not meant to suggest that Riley is not fundamentally on track. The now classic model of discussing race, under which black people are America's poster children and whites perform penance while little changes for black people who need help, has become a moral abomination. The willful neglect of the upward trajectory of black America between emancipation and the civil rights victories of the 1950s and 1960s is a grievous insult in the guise of enlightened thought. I simply submit that assigning the blame to Jesse Jackson, political opportunism, and Barack Obama's musings about how his son would have looked like Trayvon Martin may miss the targets we should be aiming at and the solutions we formulate and support.

CHAPTER 5

Black America

Changing Rhetoric into Remedies

⋑⋐

GLENN C. LOURY

JASON RILEY has written a timely and important, if somewhat depressing, essay on the present state of racial politics in America. I don't share all of Riley's political and ideological commitments. He's rather more conservative than me. I don't share his comprehensive pessimism about the welfare state. I don't agree with all of his criticisms of civil rights orthodoxy. I am less confident than he is about the likelihood that racial inequalities will naturally wither away under the beneficent influences of American capitalism.

But I do agree with Riley that advocacy on behalf of the interest of African Americans in our times is badly offtrack—intellectually, politically, and morally. I agree that the posture of today's social justice warrior—in electoral politics, in the universities, and in the media—is ill-suited to deliver genuine equality for black Americans. I agree with Riley that "culture" within some black communities is an important and detrimental influence on the life prospects of their residents.

I agree that playing "the race card" has become an impediment to honest and effective deliberations over what policies can best foster the full inclusion of blacks in the American dream. I agree that liberal Democrats often treat their black constituents in a condescending and patronizing manner— being all too ready to excuse the inexcusable and rationalize the unacceptable. I agree that racial affirmative action is no way, over the long run, to deal with underrepresentation of blacks in many elite and selective venues. I agree that our first black president, Barack Hussein Obama, did not serve well either black Americans specifically or the country as a whole with his conduct in office as it bore on the contested issues of race relations. And, perhaps most importantly, I agree that the history of blacks prior to the advent of the civil rights protests and the onset of Great Society social programs—the inspiring story of our rise from slavery and Jim Crow segregation in the first one hundred years after emancipation— offers many lessons, conservative lessons, about what it will actually take to bring about, finally, a condition of genuine equality between the races in our country. Permit me, briefly, to expand on these areas of agreement.

There are, broadly speaking, two distinct narratives available when scholars and political actors discuss the persistent subordinate economic position of African Americans in the United States today—what I'll call the *bias narrative* and the *development narrative*. The first refers to the racially discriminatory treatment of blacks; the second refers to the relative lack of investments into those activities that enhance the productivity of black Americans. (These are not mutually exclusive, of course. I do not suggest that it must be all one or the other.) Presently, the bias narrative reigns supreme, as it has done for the last fifty years. This is the so-called "civil rights vision" that the conservative black economist Thomas Sowell (cited often by Riley in this essay) so effectively criticized—to little avail—a generation ago. I share with Riley the view that this way of framing the problem is an anachronism—a hold over from the mid-twentieth century that no longer adequately captures the present-day realities for black people, especially for the most severely disadvantaged. It is a convenient anachronism, however, particularly for white liberals and for political entrepreneurs who seek to maintain their relevance and/or attract black votes.

But the plain fact of the matter is that many public policies and much public rhetoric insist on framing the problem of persistent racial inequality using this outdated mid-twentieth-century bias narrative. Additionally, they use it to prescribe remedies, as if it captures the main issues. This is a serious error in my view. For in many areas of our public life—including schools, the workplace, and the criminal justice system—the policies most likely to be effective in closing the gaps should be focused on enhancing the development of the human potential of black people and not on preventing us from being the victims of antiblack bias. Again, I do not maintain that these are mutually exclusive, that bias does not exist, or that such bias as it exists ought not to be combatted. I merely claim that it matters a great deal which narrative is emphasized, and when. This choice of narrative is enormously important. The real lives of millions of black people hang in the balance. Bad ideas can have awful consequences. To tell our people that all their woes stem from a failure of whites to treat us equally, all the while avoiding taking up the challenge of making ourselves more effective, productive, and virtuous members of society, is to take the easy path and to offer a false sense of power. It is "false black power" indeed. It is a tragic misleading of our people. And Riley is to be commended for his eloquent and passionate denunciation of this.

My own view is that we Americans—black, white, and otherwise—need a new narrative that, while remaining alert to and mindful of the problem of racially discriminatory treatment, tones down the "white supremacy has done us wrong" mantra and makes more room for a recognition of and response to the problems of inadequate human development in the African American population. This new way of thinking and talking would, among many other things, emphasize the responsibility that we blacks ourselves have— within our own families and communities—to effectively and wholeheartedly address these developmental roadblocks. This I take to be the central message of *False Black Power?* and it is spot on!

Let me give one example. Shortly after last fall's presidential election, a bot representing itself as New Jersey's (black) senator Cory Booker asked me on Facebook to sign a petition demanding that Congress nullify the Supreme Court's decision in *Shelby County v. Holder*—the case that struck down section iv(b) of the Voting Rights Act of 1965. (The result of this case was that many southern jurisdictions were relieved of a necessity to clear with the Department of Justice and the Federal Circuit Court in Washington, DC, changes in their voting laws that might have an adverse impact on black voters' electoral participation. Such changes [e.g., requiring prospective voters to present a driver's license] are said by civil rights advocates to result in racially discriminatory "voter suppression," and so on.) Upon reflection, I found myself asking (of nobody in particular): Where is the national movement going door to door to ensure that the black residents have whatever documentation they need to frustrate these Republican efforts to "disenfranchise" them? Shouldn't that be supported by millions of dollars from liberal philanthropies, by scores of black elected officials like Senator Booker himself, and by thousands of student volunteers sweeping across the southern states in a manner reminiscent of 1960s activists? Who, I wanted to ask Senator Booker's bot, will be the Bob Moses of our day? Where is the outreach, such as voter education infrastructure; promotional efforts in schools, churches, and union halls; advertising campaigns; handbills; folk songs; sermons; and calls to self-empowerment meant to foster determination and agency among the black masses (and not only in the southern states but also in the large northern cities)? Pondering these questions prompted me to feel that asking black people to straighten our metaphorical spines, to stand up and seize control of our political destinies, and to become effective political agents are the actions necessary to take us seriously. Had this been done during the 2016 election cycle in Philadelphia and Pittsburgh, in Detroit and Milwaukee, in Cleveland and Charlotte, Hillary Rodham Clinton well might have been elected president.

The fact is, there is no excuse for us black voters to remain in such a supine and infantilized state that a Republican-controlled legislature in North Carolina could neuter the political impact of black citizens merely by asking them to present an identification card. I find that entire argument to be patronizing in the extreme. How is it that the uneducated, opiate-addicted, and underemployed "deplorable" white voters who came out in droves for Donald Trump at his rallies and later in the voting booth, and who thereby elected him president, are able to pull the lever, but their black counterparts need a federal court to intervene before their political rights are validated? Our fate, I thought then and still think now, is in our own hands, not in those of a Supreme Court justice.

This is but one of many examples I could give. Liberal lamentation about the overrepresentation of blacks among those who are incarcerated seems never to get beyond accusations of racism in the criminal justice system. It should instead address the law-breaking behaviors of too many black youngsters that presaged their incarceration. Complaints that not enough black students are being enrolled in this or that college or university seem never to reach the question of the inadequate preparation of these students who rely on failing big city public school systems for their primary and secondary education. There is much talk about racial justice and virtually no talk at all about responsibility.

I share Riley's conviction about racial liberals—black, white, or otherwise—that their moral arguments are off base, that their historical interpretations are one dimensional, and that they have a shallow, parochial understanding of the country of which we are fortunate to be a part. Moreover, my antipathy and disgust toward this brand of racial liberalism are at least in part the result of the contempt I have for a feckless, trendy, sophomoric, intellectually lazy media/cultural elite—at the magazines, on social media, in broadcast journalism, and in the universities—who slavishly and uncritically repeat their party line and demand from the rest of us obeisance or, at the very least, acquiescence to their stilted narratives. As Riley insists, all of this exposes just how superficial the thinking is of those controlling the cultural megaphones of American liberalism. They can offer nothing but excuses, finger pointing, and hysteria in response to what is one of the great catastrophes of our time—namely, the failure of post-1960s progressive politics to effectively incorporate the urban black masses into the American commonwealth.

Most controversially, perhaps, I even share Riley's disappointment in the stewardship of our nation's first black president on matters related to race in America. With an eye toward his postpresidency that could well last five times longer than his time in office, Obama chose from day one to play a strategic game intended to preserve his credibility within the political/ideological matrix that constitutes modern liberalism. By doing so, an enormous opportunity was missed. Effectively leading the country on this problem required him to challenge that orthodoxy in profound ways. Instead, the opinions of an Al Sharpton weighed more heavily in his calculus than those of a Robert Woodson. Liberal attitudes on the editorial pages in New York and Washington had undue influence on his conduct. It is not only on the problem of poverty in the inner cities that our first black president provided little effective moral leadership. Consider his feckless reaction to the rioting in Ferguson and Baltimore. Recall his preemptive "if I had a son, he'd look like Trayvon" blunder (issued before any serious evaluation of the evidence in that incident was in hand, thereby contributing to the distorted narratives about that and other cases that have emerged). Teachable moments—where the true nature of these problems might have been exposed, their intractability confronted, and the inadequacies of a reflexive, tired, fifty-year-old racial liberalism revealed—were allowed to pass with the key lessons unlearned. Instead, the president and his people jumped on the racial bandwagons; they led from behind an unruly mob; they ceded the power to define these issues to demagogues, know-nothings, hustlers, and whiners. Interestingly, they could see their way clearly to taking on the "Israel Lobby" but not the Negro cognoscenti. I repeat: regarding Obama's stewardship on racial issues—for the country's sake, not that of blacks alone—I join with Riley in having nothing but contempt.

So here we are, more than a half-century past the heyday of the civil rights movement, and yet the self-appointed guardians of the interests of black America have no program, except to decry "white supremacy." They have no political vision that makes any sense to me. They offer no real solutions. They seem to have learned nothing from their failures. When addressing those who do not already agree with them (i.e., the vast majority of this great country), they have only a snarl, or a scold, or a bill of indictments to offer. We're living in a specific historical moment, a moment when the nation's discourse on racial inequality issues is being defined for generations to come. It matters a great deal whether the bias narrative or the development narrative holds sway in the decades ahead. We're in transition, as I see it, from a post-civil-rights dispensation to something else—something that will inform the nation's handling of race issues well into the future. Racial liberals have nothing constructive to say about how to manage this transition. And, while Riley himself doesn't offer many solutions in his forceful polemic, his diagnosis of what ails us is largely correct, in my view. And that's a good place to start.

CHAPTER 6

A Response to McWhorter and Loury

≥≤

JASON L. RILEY

GLENN LOURY quibbled with little that I wrote, so I'll return the favor and focus on John McWhorter's reaction.

I wish I shared McWhorter's optimism that establishment civil rights figures like Jesse Jackson and Al Sharpton are yesterday's news. Jackson may be seventy-five years old now and less publically active than in the past, but his Rainbow/PUSH organization remains influential. His Wall Street Project, which essentially shakes down large, successful businesses in the name of addressing corporate America's "racial divide," rakes in tens of millions of dollars annually. In more recent years, Jackson has taken this *de facto* extortion routine to Silicon Valley, which for the most part has paid up to make him go away. In 2015, Apple CEO Tim Cook agreed to spend some $50 million on "diversity initiatives" after meeting with Jackson.

Sharpton, for his part, has now achieved the respectability that Jackson has long enjoyed. The *New York Times* account of his sixtieth birthday bash in 2014, held in New York City's posh Four Seasons restaurant, is hard to square with McWhorter's description of an activist has-been:

> [Sharpton] has been in the news as much as ever this year, becoming a prominent advocate on behalf of the families of Eric Garner, a Staten Island man who died in police custody, and Michael Brown, the unarmed black teenager who was killed by a white police officer in Ferguson, Mo. He also has a daily platform through his show on MSNBC.
>
> Behind the scenes, he has consulted with the mayor and the president on matters of race and civil rights and even the occasional high-level appointment. He was among a small group at the White House when Mr. Obama announced his nomination of Loretta E. Lynch, the United States attorney for the Eastern District of New York, to become the next attorney general.
>
> Mr. Sharpton's newly found insider status represents a potential financial boon for him, furnishing him with new credibility and a surge in donations. His politician-heavy birthday party, at one of New York City's most expensive restaurants, was billed as a fund-raiser to help his organization. Mr. Obama also spoke at the organization's convention in April, its primary fund-raising event.[1]

What Jackson and Sharpton say and do remains relevant to our racial discussions today for at least two other reasons. First, the mainstream media continues to keep them on speed dial, as do black victims of real or imagined racial injustice. For millions of whites and for blacks of a certain age, they are still considered spokesmen for black America. The second reason they can't be ignored is that their methods have endured and they continue to inspire. The black direct protest model used today is to a significant degree their creation. The same deference that corporate America has given to Jackson is now being bestowed on the Black Lives Matter movement, whose aggressive antics and rhetoric recall Sharpton in his street-hustling days.

McWhorter says that the racial debate today has moved on for the new generation of black public intellectuals like Ta-Nehisi Coates and Michael Eric Dyson, who are making what many—though not McWhorter—see as a more sophisticated argument about what drives racial inequality. "The claim is no longer that black America owes its condition to slavery and Jim Crow," he writes. "These days—especially since the publication of William Julius Wilson's key books in the 1980s and early 1990s—the idea is that slavery and Jim Crow were followed by factory relocation, depriving poor blacks of stable, low-skill work, and red-lining, which is thought to have consigned black neighborhoods to social oblivion . . ."

McWhorter sees differences in these arguments where

I see more similarities. Whether the racism is described as overt, structural, historical, or otherwise, it is still racism that is cited as the primary culprit for group differences in outcomes. Black self-determination can be minimized, in this view, because only whites have any real agency. Perhaps more direct engagement of Wilson's writings on how the disappearance of low-skill jobs has impacted black inner cities is in order, but I don't find them any more persuasive than Coates's pleas for slavery reparations. Wilson cites the movement of jobs to the suburbs as an explanation for black inner-city social pathology. Yet the rise in black crime rates and family breakdown in the 1960s predates the job flight. Detroit and Chicago didn't riot after the factory jobs left. The riots came first. What Wilson gets right—and the reason I cite him favorably in *False Black Power?*—is that black antisocial behaviors and attitudes play a bigger role in black outcomes than most social scientists and black intellectuals want to acknowledge publically.

None of this is to say that I'm not immensely grateful for the constructive feedback and insights from John McWhorter and Glenn Loury, both of whom have spent decades writing about racial issues with logic rather than emotion as their guide. In many ways, big and small, their thinking forms the foundation upon which this work stands.

Notes

≳≲

CHAPTER 1

1. John Leland and John W. Fountain, "Film Brings in Cash and Controversy," *New York Times*, September 26, 2002.
2. Jason L. Riley, "Back Home, the Talk's Swung to Gulf," *Wall Street Journal*, March 10, 2000.
3. Ralph David Abernathy, *And the Walls Came Tumbling Down* (Chicago: Lawrence Hill Books, 2010), 470–73; Taylor Branch, *Pillar of Fire: America in the King Years, 1963–65* (New York: Simon and Schuster, 1998), 197, 207, 533.
4. Kwame Anthony Appiah and Henry Louis Gates Jr., eds., *Africana: The Encyclopedia of the African and African American Experience* (New York: Basic Books, 1999), 1499; "Browder v. Gayle: The Women Before Rosa Parks," Southern Poverty Law Center, September 2007, http://www.tolerance.org/article/browder-v-gayle-women-rosa-parks.
5. Leland and Fountain, "Film Brings in Cash and Controversy."
6. Scott Bowles, "'Barbershop' Dialogue Too Cutting, Some Say," *USA Today*, September 19, 2002.
7. Donna Britt, "Strong Enough to Survive a Few Jokes," *Washington Post*, September 27, 2002.
8. "Chicago Shooting Victims," *Chicago Tribune*, http://crime.chicagotribune.com/chicago/shootings/.
9. Edward Conlon, "The Racial Reality of Policing," *Wall Street Journal*, September 4, 2015, http://www.wsj.com/articles/the-racial-reality-of-policing-1441390980.
10. TCR Staff, "Rising Violent Crime in 13 U.S. Cities: Report," *Crime*

Report, December 20, 2016, http://thecrimereport.org/2016/12/20/violent-crime-still-up-in-many-big-cities/.

11. Alyssa Davis, "In U.S., Concern about Crime Climbs to 15-Year High," Gallup, April 6, 2016, http://www.gallup.com/poll/190475/americans-concern-crime-climbs-year-high.aspx.

12. Michael D. Shear, "Obama's 78 Pardons and 153 Commutations Extend Record of Mercy," *New York Times*, December 19, 2016, https://www.nytimes.com/2016/12/19/us/politics/obama-commutations-pardons-clemency.html.

13. "The Diversifying Electorate—Voting Rates by Race and Hispanic Origin in 2012 (and Other Recent Elections)," U.S. Census Bureau, May 2013, https://www.census.gov/prod/2013pubs/p20-568.pdf.

14. Stephan Thernstrom and Abigail Thernstrom, *America in Black and White: One Nation, Indivisible* (New York: Simon & Shuster, 1997), 140.

15. Orlando Patterson, "The Real Problem With America's Inner Cities," *New York Times*, May 15, 2015.

16. Orlando Patterson and Ethan Fosse, eds., *The Cultural Matrix: Understanding Black Youth* (Cambridge, MA: Harvard University Press, 2015), 2.

17. William Julius Wilson, "Being Poor, Black, and American: The Impact of Political, Economic, and Cultural Forces." *American Educator* (Spring 2011), http://www.aft.org/sites/default/files/periodicals/Wilson.pdf.

18. Christopher Jencks and Sara McLanahan, "Was Moynihan Right?," *Education Next* 15, no. 2 (Spring 2015), http://educationnext.org/was-moynihan-right/.

19. Ibid.

20. Erol Ricketts, "The Origin of Black Female-Headed Families," Institute for Research on Poverty, p. 32, http://www.ssc.wisc.edu/irpweb/publications/focus/pdfs/foc121e.pdf.

21. Charles Murray, *Losing Ground: American Social Policy 1950-1980* (New York: Basic Books, 1994), 115–16.

22. William Julius Wilson, *The Truly Disadvantaged: The Inner City, the Underclass, and Public Policy* (Chicago: University of Chicago Press, 1990), 3.

CHAPTER 2

1. Barry Latzer, *The Rise and Fall of Violent Crime in America* (New York: Encounter Books, 2016), 128–34.

2. "The Diversifying Electorate—Voting Rates by Race and Hispanic Origin in 2012 (and Other Recent Elections)," U.S. Census Bureau, May 2013, p. 3, https://www.census.gov/prod/2013pubs/p20-568.pdf; Linda Qiu, "Black Voter Turnout Exceeds White Voter Turnout, Even in States with Strict ID Laws, Pundit Claims," Punditfact, July 17, 2004, http://www.politifact.com/punditfact/statements/2014/jul/17/jason-ri-ley/black-voter-turnout-exceed-white-voter-turnout-eve/; Hans A. Von Spakovsky, "Clinton Gets Everything Wrong on Voting," *National Review*, June 11, 2015, http://www.nationalreview.com/article/419598/clinton-gets-everything-wrong-voting-hans-von-spakovsky.

3. Shelby Steele, *Shame: How America's Past Sins Have Polarized Our Country* (New York: Basic Books, 2015), 37–38.

4. Rachel Martin, "Selma Mayor: 'An Awesome Time for Our City,'" National Public Radio, March 8, 2015, radio broadcast, http://www.npr.org/2015/03/08/391619526/selma-mayor-an-awesome-time-for-our-city.

5. Nathan James, "Is Violent Crime in the United States Increasing?" Congressional Research Service, October 29, 2015, p. 3, https://fas.org/sgp/crs/misc/R44259.pdf; Scott Calvert, Shibani Mahtani, and Zusha Elinson, "With Their Elevated Homicide Rates, Four Cities Stand Out," *Wall Street Journal*, February 20, 2017, https://www.wsj.com/articles/with-their-rising-homicide-rates-four-cities-stand-out-1487592002.

6. German Lopez, "In Freddie Gray's Baltimore Neighborhood, Half of the Residents Don't Have Jobs," Vox, April 28, 2015, http://www.vox.com/2015/4/28/8507493/baltimore-riots-poverty-unemployment.

7. Josh Hicks and Dana Hedgpeth, "Comparing: Findings Indicate Gray Got Head Injuries in Van," NewsDiffs, April 30, 2015, http://newsdiffs.org/diff/887247/887258/; www.washingtonpost.com/local/relative-calm-on-the-streets-of-baltimore-thursday-morning/2015/04/30/65c67278-ef22-11e4-8666-a1d756d0218e_story.html.

8. Richard B. Freeman and Harry J. Holzer, "The Black Youth Employment Crisis: Summary of Findings," in *The Black Youth Employment*

Crisis, ed. Richard B. Freeman and Harry J. Holzer (Chicago: University of Chicago Press, 1986), 16; http://www.nber.org/chapters/c6281. pdf.

9. Ibid., 9.

10. Richard B. Freeman, "Cutting Black Youth Unemployment; Create Jobs That Pay as Well as Crime," *New York Times*, July 20, 1986, http://www.nytimes.com/1986/07/20/business/cutting-black-youth-unemployment-create-jobs-that-pay-as-well-as-crime.html?pagewanted=all.

11. Freeman and Holzer, "The Black Youth Employment Crisis," 15.

12. Gary Orfield and Carole Ashkinaze, *The Closing Door: Conservative Policy and Black Opportunity* (Chicago: The University of Chicago Press, 1991), 14.

13. Ibid., 7.

14. Ibid., 49.

15. United States Department of Justice, Civil Rights Division, "Investigation of the Ferguson Police Department," *Washington Post*, March 4, 2015, http://apps.washingtonpost.com/g/documents/national/department-of-justice-report-on-the-ferguson-mo-police-department/1435/.

16. Jennifer L. Hochschild, *Facing Up to the American Dream: Race, Class and the Soul of a Nation* (Princeton, NJ: Princeton University Press, 1995), 45, 48.

17. Thomas Sowell, *The Economics and Politics of Race: An International Perspective* (New York: Quill, 1983), 168–69.

18. Ibid., 32.

19. Ibid., 168.

20. Orfield and Ashkinaze, *Closing Door*, 7, 8.

21. Jennie Jarvie, "Atlanta Schools Cheating Scandal: 11 Educators Convicted of Racketeering," *Los Angeles Times*, April 1, 2015, http://www.latimes.com/nation/la-na-atlanta-school-cheating-convictions-20150401-story.html.

22. "Unemployment Rate: Black or African American," FRED Economic Data, November 2014, https://fred.stlouisfed.org/graph/?g=VoF.

23. "Unemployment Rate: Black or African American," ALFRED, February 2017, https://alfred.stlouisfed.org/series?seid=LNS14000006.

24. Valerie Wilson, "Economic Recovery for Black and Latino Workers Expands to More States in the Second Quarter of 2016," Economic

Policy Institute, August 18, 2016, http://www.epi.org/publication/economic-recovery-for-black-and-latino-workers-expands-to-more-states-in-the-second-quarter-of-2016/.

25. "Table A-2. Employment Status of the Civilian Population by Race, Sex, and Age," Bureau of Labor Statistics, last modified March 10, 2017, https://www.bls.gov/news.release/empsit.t02.htm.

26. "Labor Force Statistics from the Current Population Survey," Bureau of Labor Statistics, last modified March 25, 2017, https://data.bls.gov/timeseries/LNS11300000/

27. "Labor Force Participation Rate: Black or African American," ALFRED, February 2017, https://alfred.stlouisfed.org/series?seid=LNS11300006&utm_source=series_page&utm_medium=related_content&utm_term=related_resources&utm_campaign=alfred.

28. "Historical Poverty Tables: People and Families—1959 to 2015," U.S. Census Bureau, September 1, 2016, http://www.census.gov/data/tables/time-series/demo/income-poverty/historical-poverty-people.html.

29. Ibid.

30. Leah Binkovitz, "Employment, Income Up, According to the Latest Census Estimates," Urban Edge, September 13, 2016, https://urbanedge.blogs.rice.edu/2016/09/13/employment-income-up-according-to-the-latest-national-census-estimates/#.WJZXjlMrKM8; "Quarterly Residential Vacancies and Homeownership, Fourth Quarter 2016, U.S. Census Bureau, January 31, 2017, http://www.census.gov/housing/hvs/files/currenthvspress.pdf.

31. Bernadette D. Proctor, Jessica L. Semega, and Melissa A. Kollar, "Income and Poverty in the United States: 2015," Current Population Reports, September 2016, p. 5, https://www.census.gov/content/dam/Census/library/publications/2016/demo/p60-256.pdf; "Real Median Household Income in the United States," FRED Economic Research, 2015, https://fred.stlouisfed.org/series/MEHOINUSA672N.

32. Robert J. Barro, "The Reasons Behind the Obama Non-Recovery," *Wall Street Journal*, September 20, 2016, https://www.wsj.com/articles/the-reasons-behind-the-obama-non-recovery-1474412963.

33. Peter J. Ferrara, "Why the United States Has Suffered the Worst Economic Recovery Since the Great Depression," Heartland Institute, August 2016, pp. 2–5, https://www.heartland.org/_template-assets/

documents/publications/Ferrara%20Why%20the%20United%20States%20Has%20Suffered%20the%20Worst%20Economic%20Recovery%20Since%20the%20Great%20Depression.pdf.

34. Ibid., 5.

35. "The Employment Situation—September 2015," Bureau of Labor Statistics, October 2, 2015, https://www.bls.gov/news.release/archives/empsit_10022015.pdf.

36. "2015 State of Black America: Executive Summary and Key Findings," National Urban League, p. 6, http://soba.iamempowered.com/sites/soba.iamempowered.com/files/SOBA2015%20Executive%20Summary.pdf.

37. Jaweed Kaleem, Kurtis Lee, and Jenny Jarvie, "America Just Spent 8 Years with a Black President. For Many African Americans, It Meant One Big Thing: Freedom to 'Dream,'" *Los Angeles Times*, January 16, 2017, http://www.latimes.com/projects/la-na-obama-african-americans/.

38. Ibid.

CHAPTER 3

1. Ta-Nehisi Coates, "My President Was Black: A History of the First African American White House—and What Came Next," *Atlantic*, January/February 2017, p. 64, https://www.theatlantic.com/magazine/archive/2017/01/my-president-was-black/508793.

2. FDCH E-Media, "Transcript: Illinois Senate Candidate Barack Obama," *Washington Post*, July 27, 2004, http://www.washingtonpost.com/wp-dyn/articles/A19751-2004Jul27.html.

3. Ronald Roach, "Obama Rising: All but Assured to Become the Fifth Black American to Hold a Seat in the U.S. Senate, Obama Represents to Many the Emergence of a New Generation of National Political Leadership," *Black Issues in Higher Education* 21, no. 17 (October 7, 2004).

4. "Transcript: Obama's Commencement Speech at Morehouse College," *Wall Street Journal*, May 20, 2013, http://blogs.wsj.com/washwire/2013/05/20/transcript-obamas-commencement-speech-at-morehouse-college/.

5. William A. Darity Jr., "How Barack Obama Failed Black Americans,"

Atlantic, December 22, 2016, https://www.theatlantic.com/politics/
archive/2016/12/how-barack-obama-failed-black-americans/511358/.

6. Stuart Buck, *Acting White: The Ironic Legacy of Desegregation* (New Haven, CT: Yale University Press, 2010), 19–26.

7. John McWhorter, *Authentically Black: Essays for the Black Silent Majority* (New York: Gotham Books, 2003), 4.

8. Michael Nutter, "Speech at Mount Carmel Baptist Church," American Rhetoric, August 7, 2011, http://www.americanrhetoric.com/speeches/michaelnuttermountcarmelbaptist.htm.

9. Annette John-Hall, "In Admonishing Teen Mobs, Nutter Pulls Out Shame-Game Shackle," Philly.com, August 9, 2011, http://www.philly.com/philly/columnists/annette_john-hall/20110809_Annette_John-Hall__In_admonishing_teen_mobs__Nutter_pulls_out_shame-game_shackle.html.

10. Fredrick C. Harris, "The Rise of Respectability Politics," *Dissent*, Winter 2014, https://www.dissentmagazine.org/article/the-rise-of-respectability-politics.

11. David Remnick, "Going the Distance," *New Yorker*, January 27, 2014, http://www.newyorker.com/magazine/2014/01/27/going-the-distance-david-remnick.

12. Michael Eric Dyson, "Yes She Can," *New Republic*, November 29, 2015, https://newrepublic.com/article/124391/yes-she-can.

13. Ian Schwartz, "Cornel West on Obama: 'The First Black President Has Become the First Niggerized Black Preisdent,'" Real Clear Politics, June 22, 2015, http://www.realclearpolitics.com/video/2015/06/22/cornel_west_on_obama_the_first_black_president_has_become_the_first_niggerized_black_president.html?.

14. Eric Bates, "Beyond Hope," *New Republic*, December 13, 2016, https://newrepublic.com/article/138951/beyond-hope-barack-obama-legacy-age-trump.

15. Coates, "My President Was Black," 61.

16. Jake Tapper, "VP Biden Says Republicans 'Are Going to Put Y'all Back in Chains,'" ABC News, August 14, 2012, http://abcnews.go.com/blogs/politics/2012/08/vp-biden-says-republicans-are-going-to-put-yall-back-in-chains/.

17. "Four in Five Americans Support Voter ID Laws, Early Voting," Gallup,

August 22, 2016, http://www.gallup.com/poll/194741/four-five-amer-icans-support-voter-laws-early-voting.aspx?utm_source=tagrss&utm_medium=rss&utm_campaign=syndication; "Q: In Your View, Should Voters in the United States Be Required to Show Official, Government-Issued Photo Identification—Such as a Drivers License—When They Cast Ballots on Election Day, or Shouldn't They Have to Do This?," *Washington Post*, August 13, 2012, https://www.washingtonpost.com/page/2010-2019/WashingtonPost/2012/08/12/National-Politics/Polling/question_6226.xml?uuid=Nd4PSOTWEeGXOe75nF-yhQ.

18. Huma Kahn, Michele McPhee, and Russell Goldman, "Obama Called Police Officer Who Arrested Gates, Still Sees 'Overreaction' in Arrest," ABC News, July 24, 2009, http://abcnews.go.com/Politics/story?id=8163051&page=1.

19. Kimberly Kindy et al., "Fatal Shootings by Police Are Up in the First Six Months of 2016, Post Analysis Finds," *Washington Post*, July 7, 2016, https://www.washingtonpost.com/national/fatal-shootings-by-police-surpass-2015s-rate/2016/07/07/81b708f2-3d42-11e6-84e8-1580c7db5275_story.html?utm_term=.10d4cbb2fe21.

20. Amy L. Wax, *Race, Wrongs, and Remedies: Group Justice in the 21st Century* (Lanham, MD: Rowman & Littlefield, 2008), 91.

21. Quoctrung Bui and Amanda Cox, "Suprising New Evidence Shows Bias in Police Use of Force but Not in Shootings," *New York Times*, July 11, 2016, https://www.nytimes.com/2016/07/12/upshot/surprising-new-evidence-shows-bias-in-police-use-of-force-but-not-in-shootings.html.

22. Ronald G. Fryer Jr., "An Empirical Analysis of Racial Differences in Police Use of Force" (working paper, National Bureau of Economic Research, Cambridge, MA), 5, http://www.nber.org/papers/w22399.

23. Ibid., 6.

24. Greg Ridgeway, "Analysis of Racial Disparities in the New York Police Department's Stop, Question, and Frisk Practices," Rand Corporation, 2007, http://www.rand.org/pubs/technical_reports/TR534.html.

25. Fryer, "An Empirical Analysis of Racial Differences," 25.

26. Kent Osband, "What Statistics Say About Policing America," *Wall Street Journal*, January 4, 2015, https://www.wsj.com/articles/kent-osband-what-statistics-say-about-policing-america-1420411320.

27. Heather Mac Donald, "As Chicago Backs Off Policing, Its Murder Rate Skyrockets," Manhattan Institute, December 26, 2016, https://www.manhattan-institute.org/html/chicago-backs-policing-its-murder-rate-skyrockets-9800.html.

28. Charles Campisi, "The Myth of the Trigger-Happy Cop," *Washington Post*, February 2, 2017, https://www.wsj.com/articles/the-myth-of-the-trigger-happy-cop-1486056851.

29. Del Quentin Wilber, "Civil Rights Advocates Brace for a Radical Shift in Justice Department Priorities under Sessions and Trump," *Los Angeles Times*, November 18, 2016, http://www.latimes.com/politics/la-na-justice-department-trump-20161117-story.html.

30. Shelly Banjo, "HUD Plays Hardball with Westchester County," *Wall Street Journal*, July 15, 2011, http://blogs.wsj.com/metropolis/2011/07/15/hud-plays-hardball-with-westchester-county/.

31. Ben Wolfgang, "Obama Administration Guidelines Could Lead to Racial Quotas in School Discipline," *Washington Times*, January 8, 2014, http://www.washingtontimes.com/news/2014/jan/8/white-house-to-offer-new-rules-school-discipline/.

32. Amy Chozick and Julie Hirschfeld Davis, "Obama Sees 'Personal Insult' if Blacks Don't Rally for Hillary Clinton," *New York Times*, September 18, 2016, https://www.nytimes.com/2016/09/19/us/politics/obama-trump-clinton.html.

33. Krissah Thompson and Scott Clement, "Poll: Majority of Americans Think Race Relations Are Getting Worse," *Washington Post*, July 16, 2016, https://www.washingtonpost.com/national/more-than-6-in-10-adults-say-us-race-relations-are-generally-bad-poll-indicates/2016/07/16/66548936-4aa8-11e6-90a8-fb8Giovanni 4201e0645_story.html?utm_term=.9f540564a11b.

34. Giovanni Russonello, "Race Relations Are at Lowest Point in Obama Presidency, Poll Finds," *New York Times*, July 13, 2016, https://www.nytimes.com/2016/07/14/us/most-americans-hold-grim-view-of-race-relations-poll-finds.html.

35. William H. Frey, *Diversity Explosion: How New Racial Demographics Are Remaking America* (Washington, DC: Brookings Institution Press, 2015), 4–5.

36. Shelby Steele, "Obama's Post-Racial Promise," *Los Angeles Times*,

November 5, 2008, http://www.latimes.com/opinion/opinion-la/la-oe-steele5-2008nov05-story.html.

37. Shelby Steele, "The Exhaustion of American Liberalism," *Wall Street Journal*, March 5, 2017, https://www.wsj.com/articles/the-exhaustion-of-american-liberalism-1488751826?mod=trending_now_2.

38. Brendan Morrow, "What Groups Are Organizing the Donald Trump Protests?," Heavy, November 14, 2016, http://heavy.com/news/2016/11/what-groups-are-have-been-organizing-the-donald-trump-anti-protests-demonstrations-professional-protesters-left-wing-cities-new-york-california-portland/.

39. McWhorter, *Authentically Black*, 17.

40. Quoted in Robert E. Weems Jr., *Desegregating the Dollar: African American Consumerism in the Twentieth Century* (NY: New York University Press, 1998), 10.

41. Robert Higgs, *Competition and Coercion, 1865–1914* (Cambridge, England: Cambridge University Press, 1977), 120.

42. Robert E. Weems Jr., *Desegregating the Dollar* (NY: New York University Press, 1998), 10–13.

43. Ronald W. Bailey, ed., *Black Business Enterprise* (NY: Basic Books, 1971), 64–65.

44. Joe William Trotter, *Black Milwaukee: The Making of an Industrial Proletariat, 1915–45* (Urbana: University of Illinois Press, 1985), 80–81.

45. Booker T. Washington, *The Negro in Business* (n.p.: Hertel, Jenkins, and Co., 1907), 297.

46. Michael Javen Fortner, *Black Silent Majority: The Rockefeller Drug Laws and the Politics of Punishment* (Cambridge, MA: Harvard University Press, 2015), 41–42.

47. Martha Biondi, *To Stand and Fight: The Struggle for Civil Rights in Postwar New York City* (Cambridge, MA: Harvard University Press, 2003), 237.

48. Fortner, *Black Silent Majority* (Cambridge, MA: Harvard University Press, 2015),43.

49. Stephen Thernstrom and Abigail Thernstrom, *America in Black and White: One Nation, Indivisible* (New York: Simon and Schuster, 1997), 187–88.

50. Robert E. Weems Jr., *Desegregating the Dollar* (NY: New York University Press, 1998), 14.
51. Ibid., 72.
52. Thomas Sowell, *Black Rednecks and White Liberals* (New York: Encounter Books, 2005), 241–42.

CHAPTER 6

1. Russ Buettner, "As Sharpton Rose, So Did His Unpaid Taxes," *New York Times*, November 18, 2014, https://www.nytimes.com/2014/11/19/nyregion/questions-about-al-sharptons-finances-accompany-his-rise-in-influence.html?_r=0.

About the Contributors

GLENN C. LOURY is the Merton P. Stoltz Professor of the Social Sciences and professor of economics at Brown University. His books include *One by One from the Inside Out: Essays and Reviews on Race and Responsibility in America*; *The Anatomy of Racial Inequality*; and *Race, Incarceration, and American Values*. Among other honors, he has been elected a distinguished fellow of the American Economic Association, a fellow of the Econometric Society, a member of the American Philosophical Society, and a member of the US Council on Foreign Relations.

JOHN MCWHORTER is associate professor of English and comparative literature at Columbia University. He is the author of *The Power of Babel*, *Doing Our Own Thing*, *Our Magnificent Bastard Tongue*, *The Language Hoax*, *Words on the Move* and, most recently, *Talking Back, Talking Black*. He is a regular columnist on language matters and race issues for *Time* and CNN, writes for the *Wall Street Journal* Taste page, writes a regular column on language for the *Atlantic*, and hosts the Lexicon Valley podcast at *Slate*.

JASON L. RILEY is a senior fellow at the Manhattan Institute, a columnist for the *Wall Street Journal*, and a commentator for Fox News. He lives in suburban New York City with his wife and three children.